In Hazard

Richard Hughes
In Hazard

With an Introduction by the Author

TIME Reading Program Special Edition

Time-Life Books Inc., Alexandria, Virginia

Time-Life Books Inc.
is a wholly owned subsidiary of
TIME INCORPORATED
'TIME Reading Program: *Editor,* Max Gissen

For information about any Time-Life book, please write:
Reader Information, Time-Life Books,
541 North Fairbanks Court, Chicago, Illinois 60611

NOTE

The events in this story have been kept, to the best of my powers, strictly within the bounds of scientific possibility: the bounds of what has happened, or can happen. Nevertheless it is intended to be a work of fiction, not of history; and no single character in it is intended to be a portrait of any living person.

R. H.

RICHARD HUGHES

Editors' preface

For many years, Richard Hughes lived in a big house in Wales. Its attic, by his wife's estimate, contained some 26 wheelbarrowsful of manuscripts at one time or another. But in a writing career of more than half a century, he published only four novels.

In Hazard, which was the second, came out in 1938. Like the others, it is written in a spare, urbane, ironic prose, casting a clear dry light over a story which slips from the commonplace to extraordinary events with a baffling and delightful case.

Like the others, it starts out in a placid, matter-of-fact way. We are on board the *Archimedes*, a humdrum cargo ship on a routine voyage. We meet a Mr. Ramsay MacDonald, not the Ramsay MacDonald who in the 1920s was Britain's first Labour Prime Minister, but an elderly engineer with mustaches quite like the statesman's. We are taken on a tour of Mr. MacDonald's engine room and given a remarkably lucid account of the great, delicate devices which make a modern ship run. This particular ship is well built, well mannered, well operated, with no odder thing to meet the eye on board than the first mate's pet lemur, which nests in the foghorn and likes to hop into the rooms of sleeping deck officers and pry open their eyelids.

But it is clear from the start that something odd is about to happen—the author's very insistence on how spic-and-span, how safe and certain everything is, seems to warn us to expect the unexpected. And this is indeed an underlying theme in all of Hughes's work—how the odd, the indeterminate, the unpredictable insinuates its way into the pleasant rational little worlds that man builds for himself and turns them topsy-turvy.

Thus in his first and most famous novel, *A High Wind in Jamaica* (published in America under the title *The Innocent Voyage* because, Hughes claimed, the publishers were sure Americans thought of Jamaica only as a race track), the familiar, settled life of a family with five children is blown apart by a hurricane, and later on, the familiar, settled life of a group of pirates is wrecked by the same children, whom they have inadvertently kidnapped.

And in Hughes's third work, *The Fox in the Attic* (1961), an Englishman traveling from idyllic Wales to pastoral Bavaria in the peaceful year 1923 gradually finds his life entwined with that of several wretched little provincials, one of them named Adolf Hitler, who are about to tear the whole modern world loose from its moorings. (*The Fox in the Attic* was the first book of an unfinished trilogy; the second book, *The Wooden Shepherdess*, appeared in 1973.)

The action of *In Hazard* gets its twist into the unexpected from a storm which makes the Jamaican high wind seem like a breeze. It is in fact the greatest tropical storm on record, sending the barometer down to a low of 26.99, and it comes howling down one November day, while the *Archimedes* is plodding carefully and correctly across the Caribbean. Within a few hours the powerful engines are at a standstill, and the sturdy ship, constructed to withstand any imaginable stress from the elements, is wallowing like a sodden log, broadside to mountainous seas in a 200-mile-an-hour wind, with no electricity, no steam, no way to steer, no way to call for help, no food, no water to drink. A crew carefully trained to handle the complex problems of modern sea travel has to cope with the more elemental ones of survival.

Any book on such a theme naturally invites comparison with Joseph Conrad's classic tale of the sea, *Typhoon*. Hughes has gone out of his way to underscore the similarities, as if deliberately challenging the old master on his own ground. Of course all great storms have a certain family resemblance. But the human elements on Hughes's *Archimedes* have remarkable parallels to those on Conrad's *Nan-Shan*. The skipper on each is a solid, unimaginative man who rises to unexpected heights in response to overwhelming challenge. Younger officers on both ships take a step into manhood as they learn something of

courage and despair and endurance. There are pan-
icky Chinese coolies in one ship, sullen Chinese crew-
men in the other, uncomprehending and miserable in
both ships.

If anything, Hughes is more ambitious than Conrad. Not only is his storm the longer, lasting four days
to the other's two; he has more characters, he probes
more deeply into the social structure on board ship,
and he carries his story further in time, both forward
and backward. Toward the end, in fact, he almost
stretches the structure of his novel to the breaking
point by including the life story of one of the Chinese
seamen: not a nameless coolie but a vereran of Mao
Tse-tung's early armies, a peasant boy turned disciplined Communist, whose fate links up the physical
tempest in the West Indies with the historical storm
of revolution then—in the 1930s—beginning to con-
vulse the world.

But the heart of both books remains the descrip-
tion of the storm itself, and here Hughes has nothing
to yield to Conrad or to any other writer of the sea.
No wind in literature blows so salt and blinding
into the reader's eyes as the one that pounds the
Archimedes.

A deftly controlled realism gives extraordinary
power to Hughes's descriptive and dramatic scenes
alike. He shifts effortlessly from over-all views—the
mechanics of the storm, the battering and crippling
of the ship—to vivid details of men on board as they

flounder through efforts, always dangerous, mostly futile, to get things going again.

In the mad onrush of the storm, detail after detail flies by, confusedly and terrifyingly. The giant waves are "the size and almost the shape of trees—trees galloping about, lashing and thrashing each other to bits." The Chinese deckhands are "piled up, like a pile of half-dead fish on a quay." To the men on the listing deck, "the horizon tilted sideways," looking as if it were about to slide onto the decks an ocean full of expectant sharks. At the dead center of the hurricane, a freak of the winds covers the whole ship with all kinds of winged things, from grasshoppers to herons, and officers walking barefoot on the deck feel the horrible crunch of little bones as they keep stepping on birds stuck on the oily metal: "no bird, even crushed, or half-crushed, cried."

The apocalyptic images of external nature merge with the human drama inside the ship. Hughes, who offers a new and fascinating explanation of the book in an introduction written for this special edition, once denied that the novel was about a storm at all: it was about fear. There is fear all through the ship, a "bitter, ammoniac" smell of it. It takes many forms, from the abject animal panic of the supernumerary officer, Mr. Rabb, burrowing under a huddling mass of wretched, seasick Chinese sailors, to the boyish hallucinations of the young deck officer, Mr. Watchett, trapped in his room by the wind and fighting claustrophobia in the darkness by alternate communication with God and, in his memory, with the naked body of the Southern belle who collapsed stone drunk at his feet only a couple of days before at a gay party in Norfolk, Virginia.

Along with the fear goes the transcendence of fear: courage, laconic, understated and matter-of-fact in the best British tradition. There are the engineers who crawl into the stokehold, inches below the great flames shooting out of the furnaces, "like chops under a gas-grill," in the hopeless effort to get the engines under control, and who later break into obsessive Scotch wranglings on metaphysics and the afterlife. There is Captain Edwardes, an unimpressive, "rather cherubic" person who, when things began to look really bad, "knew that the men needed some encouragement; so he gave it."

It is the welding of all these details which gives the characteristic note of Hughes's novels—the note of veracity. We have the assurance that however out-of-the-ordinary the situation may be, this is what things must be like in such a situation.

Not that the author had physically been on the spot, with a notebook in his hand. He never went through a world's-record typhoon, any more than Conrad did. As he says in the introduction, he only heard about a ship that had been through an appalling storm, and the story unaccountably fascinated him. He read the log of the ship, interviewed men who had been on board, shipped on a freighter himself so that he could get a below-decks slant on things. Then he set to work for four years, writing and rewriting. This process has always taken him a long time, he once explained, because "I write short books. That means writing slowly. It is what you leave out of a book which takes the time, not what you put in."

When *In Hazard* appeared in 1938 it was widely—almost unanimously—applauded. "The most outrageous quality of *In Hazard*," wrote an admiring Graham Greene, "is...its daring—to take the same subject as Conrad in *Typhoon*, the simple story of a hurricane and human endurance, to include even a shipload of Chinese; it would be foolhardy if it were not triumphantly justified." The book has been translated into every European language.

Hughes, for all his scanty production, had been writing since childhood—in fact, it might be said, since before he could write: at five he dictated poems to his mother. He attended Oxford and while there wrote regularly for various British journals. In addition to his novels, he published two books of poems, a book of short stories and two children's books; he also had four plays produced in Britain. George Bernard Shaw said that one of them was the best one-act play ever written.

He is often thought of as an exotic writer, but he was really one of the most down-to-earth. He had a piratical look about him, and he enjoyed his share of tramping about the world, forming friendships with

Moroccan chieftains and Balkan rebels and such; the way to travel, he claimed, was to take off with just enough money for your voyage out and depend on your imagination to get you back. He picked up many out-of-the-way impressions and landscapes as a result, but his strength as a writer was that the exotic, being perfectly familiar to him, became thoroughly domesticated in his work. His characters go off to distant climes and they get themselves caught in the unlikeliest complications, but they are instantly recognizable as real human beings, fellow sharers with us all in "The Human Predicament"—a rather grandiose phrase which Hughes selected as a title for the series of novels on which he was working at the time of his death in 1976.

—THE EDITORS

®️ Introduction

When this novel was first published, the line taken in a brief prefatory note was this: "The events in this story have been kept...strictly within the bounds of scientific possibility: the bounds of what has happened, or can happen...."

That note, which is also found in this edition, was written a long time ago. There were good reasons then for this mere half-truth; but today there can be none for not being more explicit. This *is* a novel, a story about people who never existed; but the whole inanimate side of it is fact.

Once, in recent meteorological history, there really had been a hurricane as stupendous and as unpredicted as the one here recorded, and a British cargo steamer very like the *Archimedes* did live through it— just. Day by day, hour by hour, minute by minute that storm did behave in detail as is here narrated.

But there fact ends. For purposes of my novel I signed on a new and wholly imaginary crew. There are no *human* portraits here, for this would neither have been decent behavior to the men themselves nor would it have served my purposes as a novelist.

I examined that steamer from stem to stern while a crusted water line (from the 1,000 tons of sea she had shipped), slanting diagonally up the bulkheads dividing her holds, was still there to prove the incredible angle of the list she had taken and how near she had been to filling; while one could still see and handle cold steel torn and twisted like paper, tangled like string. I studied her logs and track charts. I questioned deck officers and engineers while their experience was still liquid in them so that, however reticent their normal natures, for the time being they could not help but talk and talk and talk. A little later, and in another command, I went to sea with her master. Thus I was able to piece together their several stories until possessed of the complete narrative of everything which had happened, in the material sense, in every several part of her: until I knew more about the total effects of that wind than any one of them separately knew.

How did I get this rare chance? The answer is simple: her owners felt that an event so extraordinary must never be forgotten. They had sent for me, as for some kind of tribal bard.

But why did I jump at the chance when I got it?

Here the answer is much less simple. I was already in the throes of another novel which this new project would have to elbow into limbo. The book moreover would be utterly unlike anything else I had written or expected to write—or, indeed, was fitted by experience to write, for I had never been to sea in steam (any more than, before writing *A High Wind in Jamaica*, I had ever been a little girl). The work involved would be immense. Why, then, this interest in an alien and merely true event so compulsive that I felt under the Muse's explicit orders to drop everything else and write it?

At the time of writing I was only aware of the compulsion: I had no glimmer of a notion *why*. Now, looking back, I do think I begin to see at least one reason. But to explore it calls for some rather recondite delving into the general motivation of imaginative writing; and perhaps at this point even the thoughtful reader (the other sort skips introductions anyway) would rather turn on to the story itself.

He will find a plain sea story about men in a storm (it is quite short and, although it took four years to write, can be read at a sitting). He can then come back, if he still wants to, abler to judge whether what follows here has a likely ring; but unless he has a real lust for taking the lids off writers to see how the wheels go round he had better not come back at all, for he may find what follows a rather rarefied and theoretical introduction to any plain sea story about men in a storm!

My own inclination in any such inquiry is to start from the premise of those who hold (the young Robert Graves was among the first to suggest it) that the writing of poetry does for the poet what dreaming does for Tom, Dick and Harry: it allows a safe outlet for conflicts and tensions too painful for his conscious mind to face, disguised so impenetrably in symbol that the poet himself has no inkling of what his poem is really "about"—just as the dreamer has none till his analyst tells him. The tension both determines the symbol and generates the compulsive force. Moreover, let me stress from the start the fundamental difference between symbol (in this dream sense) and conscious allegory: the poet's absolute ignorance of what he is really saying seems to be necessary if the magic is to work. A classic example is Keats's *La Belle Dame sans Merci;* the poet's agonized mind has palpably fused Fanny Brawne and Consumption in a single image, yet his own comments at the time (and his revisions are even more symptomatic) seem to show him quite unaware of this at a conscious level.

Usually these same critics (again with Robert Graves among the most emphatic) downright deny the same to be true of prose, that the roots of a prose piece ever run right down "under the threshold" as poetry does. But why? If an imaginative prose work has also insisted on being written—in its humbler way yet still just as irresistibly as a hen's egg insists on being laid—why must the novelist's compulsion be assumed to differ in kind from the poet's? An almost instantaneous flash of lightning and the steady illumination of a lamp are both electric light.

xviii

Mostly these multiple generating tensions are private and personal, like Keats's; and in this field, I should probably be the last to know even today what private neuroses of my own saw themselves reflected in these twin symbols of ship and hurricane, or constructed this varied picture of men enduring prolonged inanimate danger to be their escape hatch. But tensions can also derive from the situation of a whole society, and it is here that I think I do begin to see daylight.

For the period when this hurricane story reached and so instantly obsessed me was those early 1930s when the fading smell of remembered death in Britain was just beginning to be replaced by a new stench that was death prefigured. War, we had thought till then, was so safely behind us—the Great War, the "war to end all wars"; for more than 12 years we had been believing that with this final holocaust civilized man had worked war right out of his system. Indeed to many it had seemed an overinsurance that we had even bothered to set up a League of Nations at all, with adequate powers to withstand any risk of war in the impossible event that risk arose! When, step by step, that old postwar world was changed under our eyes into a new prewar one, how *could* we believe it? Reason forbade (for in really important matters Reason always is nine parts wishful thinking).

In 1931, Japan invaded Manchuria and the League failed to stop it. In 1933, Hitler came to power and began to rearm. The next year, his abortive coup in Austria meant that henceforth Mussolini was needed on the Brenner Pass, and Italian designs on Abyssinia had to be winked at. But in Manchuria, we told ourselves, white men weren't involved (and yellow men are a different species from ours—don't quite count). As for Germany rearming, surely she'd a right to resume her place among the Powers, and this would content her? Abyssinia involved only one European nation, so still hardly counted. Spain, then, where white men did fight each other? We were knowing enough Freudians by now to see Spain as a grim football ground where (for the better security of world peace) the Communist and Fascist Powers could sublimate in semiprivate.

Right till the end all 10 parts of Reason went on telling us the final cataclysm would be dodged. Even in the summer of 1938, when Chamberlain waved "Peace in Our Time" in our faces, most of us believed him—or thought we did. "Or *thought* we did"—for that is the point I am making, that all this time, the bottoms of our minds knew better; that in our bones we had foreseen from the very beginning this hurricane of preternatural power which no maneuvering could dodge. Under this threshold of consciousness we were well aware that it would prove worse than even imagination could envisage but that we should endure, somehow reviving in ourselves that trust in stubbornness and Providence supposedly long since leached out.

When Reason plays the deaf adder—one ear in the sand and her tail plugging the other then only symbol can serve; and a true-life story serves best of all as symbol, since even the inward censor has to admit its "truth." Moreover, the text bristles with clues (which is typical of the workings of the subconscious): for example, how could I have written even that first page of the book without recognizing what my "ship" really stood for? Certainly no dream-analyst could.

Of course, had this been allegory and a conscious attempt to foretell the future couched in the terms of allegory, then I could claim to be a prophet of no mean rank: for little ingenuity would be needed to read into the story not only a foretelling of the onset of the war and its violence but even details of its future course—right down to the final *American* salvage ship! But that would be to misread it entirely, since this is not allegory at all but symbol; and symbol (in the dream sense) is never concerned primarily with the future *qua* future but with a much more timeless kind of truth.

All the same, this brings me to my final point: my symbol's eventual impact on my readers.

Till now, we have been concerned only with those motions in the writer's mind which went to make the book. But our initial premise can be applied also to those motions in the reader's mind to which a poem or a book gives rise. For where some tension in the writer's mind has eased itself in symbol, then that symbol may couple itself to a like tension in the reader or even (for that is the ambiguous nature of symbol) to some wholly different one. Indeed, perhaps the real reason we like reading is to have our therapeutic dreaming supplied us, thus, from outside.

It follows that at times of exceptionally deliberate self-deception people tend to shun all poetry and fiction; indeed it is symptomatic of a fear of the naked truth to prefer nonfiction.

From these last two paragraphs, what happened when the book first appeared, and again a little later, can perhaps be imagined. For it was published in 1938. The literary notices it got could hardly have been better, but initially it failed entirely to excite the general reader as, nine years earlier, *A High Wind in Jamaica* had done. For this was Munichtime, and people had something other than mere novels to think about—or supposed they had; and anyway, here was Chamberlain back from Germany with the blessed news that the hurricane *had* been dodged!

Thus initial sales were merely respectable. But when war after all did come and disaster followed disaster, something rather curious happened. Without being any more talked-about than before (for I doubt if readers knew why they were reading it any more than the writer had known why he wrote it), the book became more and more widely read. When at last the war was over and the British publisher checked his sales figures, he rubbed his eyes:

he could hardly believe that in fact his sales of this book by that time had actually outstripped his total sales of the far more widely talked-of earlier one—in spite of paper-rationing and all.

So let me sum up, thus: I believe the theme of this book and of the "historical novel of my own times" I am engaged on now to be fundamentally the same. But what *The Fox in the Attic* (and the succeeding volumes still to come) looks at consciously with hindsight, *In Hazard* had already looked at 30 years ago quite unconsciously—with foresight.

—RICHARD HUGHES

Part I

Chapter I

Amongst the people I have met, one of those who stand out the most vividly in my memory is a certain Mr. Ramsay MacDonald. He was a Chief Engineer: and a distant cousin, he said, of Mr. J. Ramsay MacDonald, the Statesman. He resembled his "cousin" very closely indeed, in face and moustaches; and it astonished me at first to see what appeared to be my Prime Minister, in a suit of overalls, crawling out of a piece of dismantled machinery with an air of real authority and knowledge and decision.

For it was in 1924 (during the first Labour Government), that I originally met Mr. MacDonald: in the "Archimedes," a single-screw turbine steamer of a little over 9,000 tons.

She was a fine ship. Purely a cargo-vessel (unless you refuse to class as cargo the Moslem pilgrims she occasionally carried). Her owners, one of the most famous Houses in Bristol, had a large fleet;

but they loved each vessel and got the utmost out of her as if she was their child—a deep, sincere, selfish love like that, not mere sentiment. They built their ships to their own designs. They kept them in perfect repair, never hesitating to scrap anything that was antiquated or insecure. They never insured them. If there was any loss, it should be as much their own as the gains. There was a fanatical determination against any risk of loss, therefore, in everyone from the Chairman of the Company to the Ship's Cat.

No caution could be too great. Look at the funnel-guys of the "Archimedes," for instance. They were designed to stand a strain of a hundred tons! But how could a strain of a hundred tons ever come upon funnel-guys? A wind of seventy-five miles an hour would blow every shred of canvas out of a sailing ship; yet even such a hurricane, the designers reckoned, would only lean against the funnel of "Archimedes" with a total pressure of ten or fifteen tons. The funnel itself (there was an inner one and an outer one bracketed together) was rigid enough to stand any such ordinary strain alone. When these guys were properly set up, that funnel was as safe as the Bank of England.

II

Mr. MacDonald, I think I said, was Chief Engineer. He was monarch of the engine-room, the fire-room, and various outlying territories.

The Beginning

An engine-room is unlike anything in land architecture. It is an immensely tall space—reaching from the top of the ship, more or less, to the bottom. Huge. But, unlike most large architectural spaces (except perhaps Hell), you enter it through a small door at the top.

Its emptiness is most ingeniously occupied by carefully placed machines: high and low pressure turbines, reduction gear, condensors, pumps and so on. But the visitor, of course, sees nothing of the nature of these machines, each being securely buttoned up in an iron case, with hundreds of heavy iron bolts for buttons. Large pipes of varying widths, some of them—cold—of shining bedewed copper, and others wrapped in thick white clothing to keep in their heat, connect one with another.

You have seen, in a bush on a foggy day, the spider-runs among the branches? So, too, in an engine-room there are little metal runs at different levels, and gossamer steel stairs, to carry you to whatever part you want of these huge iron lumps: and above you are cranes and overhead railways to convey tools and spare parts for you, since such tools and spare parts often weigh several tons.

The polished steel handrails are slippery with oil and moisture. The air, too, is a contrast to the bright sea-air outside: it is warm, and softened with steam (for a little always manages to escape from somewhere): and the place is moderately loud with the clangour of machinery.

In Hazard

The stokehold (or fire-room), which you enter at the bottom ordinarily, through a low door from the bottom of the engine-room, is a very different place. The air here is hotter still; but quite dry. Here, moreover, is a symmetry more like that of land-architecture: a row of similar furnaces, small at the bottom and growing larger above, so that overhead they tend to come together, like gothic arches in a metal crypt (or the walls of a room in a dream).

Opposite you, as you enter from the engine-room, is a line of oven-like doors, each with a little spy-hole bright with the flames within. As you peer in through one of these holes at all that raging fire, it is hard to believe that it comes from the burning of only one little jet of hot oil, squirted through a nipple small enough to carry in a waistcoat pocket! And at the side of each furnace door is a container, such as you might stand an umbrella in. It holds a torch—a long iron rod with a bundle of rags at the end, immersed in oil. To relight a furnace (while it is still warm), all you need to do is to turn very carefully two cocks, one supplying the hot oil and the other a forced draught of air: and then a China-man lights the torch and thrusts it through a small hole into the empty, oven-like hollow of the furnace, where the hot oil vapor bursts immediately into a roaring flood of flame.

Here, of course—in the fire-room—you are directly under the roots of the funnel. A steel ladder leads up into the space around its base, which is known as the Fiddley: and a doorway there gives direct access on to the deck for those firemen whose turn it is to enjoy a little fresh air: but the visitor to whom Mr. MacDonald is showing his regions generally passes back into the engine-room again.

And there, beyond all this vastness of furnaces and clanging machinery, you will find at last the quiet, simple thing that all this is about: namely, a smooth column of steel, lying in cool and comfortable bearings and turning round and round with no sound—the propeller-shaft. A passage in which you cannot quite stand upright conveys its great length to the tail of the ship.

Think of a tree. The roots of a tree spread in a most complicated manner through the ground, extracting all kinds of necessary things. This nourishment passes, unified, up the plain column of its trunk, and bursts out in the air into a countless multitude of leaves. So all the varying forces, the stresses and resistances, proceeding from that welter of machinery, are unified into the simple rotation of this horizontal column: are conducted calmly along its length into the sea: and there burgeon suddenly into the white and glass-green foliage of the swirls, the tumbling currents, the enormously powerful jostling of crowded water which is a ship's wake.

In Hazard

III

All that belonged exclusively to Mr. MacDonald, and so did certain other isolated mechanisms in the ship. The steering-gear, for instance, in its "house" on the after-castle (in the stern). That is a massive engine: yet its powerful forces, shifting with exactitude the heavy rudder, can be switched on or off by the delicate wrist of a Chinese quartermaster on the bridge, lightly twiddling the wheel. And should the wheel on the bridge for any reason be out of action, there is a second, an emergency wheel in the stern which can be connected up. But should the steam steering-engine itself fail, why, then you would be in a hole. For you cannot move so heavy a rudder by hand. Not all the man-power in the ship would suffice to move it one inch.

What else shall I tell you, to describe to you "Archimedes"? I say nothing of her brilliant paint-work, or the beauty of her lines: for I want you to know her, not as a lover knows a woman but rather as a medical student does. (The lover's part can come later.)

Here is some more. The hull of a ship is double, and the space between the two skins is divided into compartments. It is these compartments in the actual walls of the ship which are called the tanks. They serve several purposes. Some contain the fuel oil ("Archimedes" being an oil-burning steamer). Others, if the sea is admitted to them, can be made to act as ballast, to control and adjust the stability

8

of the ship. Others contain the fresh water. Access to these tanks can be had through man-holes, some of which are in the engine-room floor: and they are ventilated (fuel-oil gives off explosive gases) by some of those hook-topped pipes that you may have noticed on the promenade-deck of a liner, near the rails. It is the ship's carpenter's job to sound all these tanks once every watch, and record exactly the depth of whatever is in them.

So much, then, for Mr. MacDonald's region. He had under him seven engineer officers, their tartarean occupation indicated by a shred of purple against the gold on their sleeves: and under them was a sensible and skilful crew of Chinese firemen and greasers. The rest of the ship—the hull, the decks, and chiefest of all the cargo-space—belonged to Mr. Buxton, the Chief Officer, *alias* First Mate.

It is curious how little interest deck-officers and engineers (of the old school) take in each other's provinces. It is not so much a tactful avoidance of trespass as a complete ignoring. The engineer has to make certain machines work, but he has no interest whatever in what they are used for. He is as careless where they take him as a man's stomach is careless on what errand his legs are bound. The deck officer, for his part, hardly seems to know whether he is on a motor-ship or a steamer (except by the amount of dirt on the decks). He cannot explain the working of any simple mechanism that he employs every day. In their lives, too, they are segregated, as completely as boys and girls are in British education.

Even in the "Archimedes," where the policy was to throw them together, it did not really work. In the shipshape, decent mahogany of the Officers' Saloon they dined at separate tables, the apprentices' table as a barrier between them. Their quarters were separate. Even the Chinese firemen slept at one end of the ship, and the Chinese deckhands at the other!

There are, of course, certain parts of the ship where the frontier is rather hard to draw—but drawn it is, everywhere. The inside of the funnel, for instance, belonged to Mr. MacDonald, the outside to Mr. Buxton. The steam-whistle belonged to Mr. MacDonald, but the foghorn unquestionably lay in the province of Mr. Buxton. This last point was not, in the "Archimedes," so unimportant as it sounds. For it happened that Mr. Buxton had a slow-moving lemur, a "Madagascar Cat," called Thomas; and it was in the foghorn that he habitually slept through the hours of daylight. He had the right to, seeing it was under his master's rule. It was his sanctuary.

This little Thomas slept all day, and he was not very energetic even at night. But he had one prejudice. He liked the human eye, and he did not approve of it being shut, ever. If he came into Mr. Buxton's cabin while his master was asleep he would jump carefully on to the edge of the bunk, and then with anxious and delicate movements of his long fingers he would lift the sleeping man's eyelids till the ball was fully exposed. This he would do to other deck-officers too, if he found them (to his distress) with their eyes shut at night upon any excuse whatever. They had, of course, to put up with Thomas (if the night was too hot to shut their doors): it was a matter of discipline. A woman in English society takes the rank of her husband: and at sea a pet takes the rank of its owner. An insult to the Chief Officer's lemur would be an insult to the Chief Officer.

As for the Engineers, Thomas knew well enough that he must never so much as approach their quarters: and in his master's foghorn no-one dared to touch him.

IV

In the late summer of 1929 (five years after my first meeting with Mr. MacDonald) the "Archimedes" took in a mixed cargo at various ports on the Atlantic seaboard, for the Far East. The elaborate matter of its stowage Mr. Buxton was responsible for, of course (a deck officer has actually to know more about cargo than about waves). At New York he stowed some bags of wax at the bottom. Then came many kinds of mixed whatnots. One item was a number of tons of old newspapers, which the Chinese like to build their houses of. These were mostly stowed in the 'tween-decks—high up, that is to say, since they were comparatively light. At Norfolk (Virginia) they took in some low-grade tobacco, also bound for China, where it would be made into cheap cigarettes. This too was stowed in the 'tween-decks.

Norfolk was the last loading port, and they were delayed there a bit. This was not irksome, however. Philadelphia, in spite of the stink in the docks, had been all right in its way since most of the officers had friends there; but Norfolk far outdid even Philadelphia in hospitality. The Master and the Chief Officer (it is a rule) must never both go ashore at the same time. Yet at Norfolk there were so many parties that both could have their fill of pleasure. Even Mr. MacDonald, when he could be persuaded to go to one of these affairs, grew gay—or at least, gayish.

The junior officers mostly attended other and more casual parties, at which they had many eye-opening experiences. Mr. Watchett, for instance, of the sober East Anglian market-town of Fakenham, a very young officer, was caught up suddenly one night by a troop of Southern boys and girls. He told them he came from Norfolk, England— it was enough introduction. He had never seen them before that minute, but they treated him at once with the kindly indifference of old friends. They danced his legs off, somewhere; and then suddenly crowded into cars, and drove out into the night. The hot smell of oiled, sandy roads: the very high trees almost meeting overhead: the din of frogs and insects. They arrived at a fine Colonial house and gave Dick Watchett corn-whisky in a room full of elaborate Victorian-looking furniture that smelt musty.

They were all highly civilised. Amongst them was one older man, an ex-soldier. He wore a gilt and ormolu leg with his evening clothes, for he held that the merely serviceable artificial limb which he wore with his day-clothes was wrong with a tuxedo. There was also in the party one very lovely fair girl, with wide innocent eyes. She was in the first bud of youth—still at High School. She told Dick that she came of a peculiarly aristocratic family, the property of whose blood, for countless generations, had been to send any flea which bit them raving mad. This property, indeed, had been their ruin. For her father, in order to win a footling bet, had wantonly deranged the wits of some of the most valuable performers in a flea-circus: and the family plantation had to be mortgaged to pay the enormous damages which the Court awarded against him. At least, so she told Dick.

This was the first inkling which Dick Watchett had that America, as well as Europe, held her ancient aristocratic families, jealous of their blood.

The man with the gilt and ormolu leg kept trying to make love to this girl (whose name was Sukie). She resented it, being actually as innocent even as she looked: so she adopted Dick as her protector, nestling against him like a bird. He did not notice that she was drinking far more neat corn-whisky even than he drank himself. Actually it was more than she was used to, being so young, and this her first party of the kind also: but having begun it did not occur to her to stop. It arrived in glass jars, each holding a gallon: so there was plenty.

Presently she told Dick she had a cat so smart that it first ate cheese and then breathed down the mouseholes—with baited breath—to entice the creatures out. Her eyes were getting very wild: and sometimes, as she lay in Dick's arm, she shivered. Dick did not try to talk to her much: but he enjoyed her being there. His own head was a little giddy, and the party seemed to advance and recede, and was difficult to listen to. But Sukie, by then, must have drunk quite a pint of the bootleg liquor neat, which is a lot for a girl of sixteen: and in time it took hold of her altogether. She suddenly struggled out of his arms, and sprang to her feet. Her eyes, wider than ever, did not seem to see anybody, even him. She wrenched at her shoulder-straps and a string or two, and in a moment every stitch of clothing she had was gone off her. For a few seconds she stood there, her body stark naked. Dick had never seen anything like it before. Then she fell unconscious on the floor.

Dick set down his own drink suddenly, a wilder intoxication thumping in his ribs. She had been lovely in her clothes, but she was far more lovely like this, fallen in a posture as supple as a pool; all that white skin; her forlorn little face, with its closed eyes, puckered already in the incipient distress of nausea. Suddenly Dick realised that everyone else had left the room: and as suddenly he realised that he loved this girl more than heaven and earth. With shaking hands he rolled her in the hearth-rug, for fear she should catch cold: made her as comfortable as he could on a sofa; and returned, shaking, to his ship.

For hours he lay awake, quite unable even to dim the vivid picture in his inward eye of Sukie's drunken innocence. But at last he fell asleep, her lovely face and her naked body flickering in his dreams. And then presently he was awakened by feeling his heavy lids lifted by thin little fingers, and found himself staring, through the texture of his dream, into large, anxious, luminous eyes, only an inch from his own; eyes that were not Sukie's. He bashed at the electric light switch in a panic.

It was Thomas, with his soft fur and his big tail, hopping away on his unnaturally elongated feet, nervously folding and unfolding his ears.

The next night, the night before their departure for Colon and the Panama Canal, Captain Edwardes gave a party on board, with dancing to a gramophone. The gramophone belonged to Mr. Foster, the Second Mate. The ladies were friends of the Captain's: relatives of the company's agent chiefly, or of the shippers. They were picked by the dictates of duty. None of them were young, and none beautiful: and not being aristocratic like Dick's friends, they behaved with a strict but slightly coarse decorum. Captain Edwardes himself, Mr. Buxton, and Mr. MacDonald, were as happy and as flirtatious as children, and the dance went on till very late—till nearly half past eleven.

The only officer who did not take part was Mr. Rabb. Mr. Rabb did not belong in the "Archimedes": he was down as a Supernumerary Officer, not as a numbered mate. He really belonged to the "Descartes"—another of the Sage Line's fleet of philosophers: and was to be landed at Colon to join her.

Mr. Rabb was a strict Christian, and did not really approve of dancing under any conditions. But especially he thought it wrong on the part of senior officers with impressionable young juniors in their charge. Apart from the four apprentices, who were still boys, there was Dick Watchett, for instance. To dance with these ladies might well arouse in him those very passions from which a life at sea was intended by God as a refuge. Watchett showed very little outward sign of being inflamed by holding any of these partners in his arms; yet it was against nature that he should in fact not be —who knew that better than Mr. Rabb? And the young are so deceitful.

The Beginning

However, it was not his business: this was not even his ship. But he hoped Captain Theobald, of the "Descartes," would prove more serious-minded.

Dick Watchett liked Mr. Rabb, as did all juniors who came in contact with him. The midshipmen adored him. And indeed he was a likeable person, with his crisp hearty voice, his clean mind, and his courteous manner with the young or the poor—the best type of Englishman.

Chapter II

"Archimedes" left Norfolk at four the next afternoon, passing down the Elizabeth river into Hampton Roads. Craney Island Lighthouse—thought Dick Watchett—looked like a Swiss Châlet on stilts. The yellow shore was low and flat, with sandy beaches: the Roads full of traffic—Bay steamers, chiefly, and long strings of lighters.

By half past six they were off Cape Henry, and there dropped the pilot.

Vessels bound south keep close to Cape Henry, inside the banks. It is a strange coast, from there down to Cape Hatteras; most of it just a low stretch of beach dividing the inland waters from the ocean: a rather vague limit for so great a continent. That far, Captain Edwardes's course lay inshore. But south of Cape Hatteras the coast falls away to the westward: at Cape Hatteras, therefore, at three in the morning, "Archimedes" said goodbye to North America, shaping a course for the West Indian island of San Salvador.

18

The Beginning

That day was fine and clear. The sea and sky were a dark blue, the few clouds white and fleecy. Although it was now late autumn, summer seemed to have returned. For, once they were through the Gulf Stream, the sun, undeterred by cloud or mist, made up for the lateness of the season by the strength a southern latitude lent it. "Archimedes" was alone in the sea, and land newly forgotten —that time when everyone in a ship is at his happiest.

Alone, that is to say, except for the dolphins. For the stem of the ship, cutting through the violet glass, tossed glittering piles of the whitest foam outwards: and deep in the heart of that glass the dancing dolphins were the most beautiful thing I had ever seen. A dozen, huge ones, much longer than men; the colour of their backs an olive brown, their sides and bellies a pale and shining green: their shapes the very shape of Speed itself. The pointed nose, in front of the swelling forehead, opened the water perfectly; and it slid together again behind the throbbing tail as if they had been nothing.

Mostly they danced in twos, swinging from side to side of the stem like two people skating together: then crossing, one over, the other under: then rolling over and over sideways, a flash of greenish silver deep under the water: rising to the surface, so that the back fin cut the air with a white plume: leaping into the air like powerful mermaids too happy to lie still: leaping, twisting on to their backs as they leapt, sometimes two, sometimes three, or four or five together. Two would suddenly swing away, and altogether leave the ship: two more from nowhere cross the bows and join in the heavenly water-play.

At first Sukie had blazed in Dick's mind, lighting every part of it: but now already, after two days, she had contracted and receded like the opening by which you have entered a tunnel: turned more unearthly bright than the broad day, but very distant and small and clear. Yet now, as he watched the dolphins, for a moment light seemed to come back over his whole mind, gently flooding all its dark places, and then fading in a mood of pleasurable sadness.

Again that night he saw something very beautiful: something seldom seen (except in the China Seas): a patch of ocean so phosphorescent that it cast a glow into the sky before they reached it. As they came to it, the whole water sparkled like stars, and everything that moved in it was sheathed in cold flame. Deep beneath it some fish sent out a rotating light, like a lighthouse.

It was a rare and magnificent thing. But it did not move him as the naked dolphins had done.

II

It took them four days to reach San Salvador.

They seemed now to have passed through the

little oasis of summer: it was succeeded by a grey, south easterly swell, and a fresh breeze; and the weather was cloudy, with occasional showers. But there was no reason to expect really bad weather: the hurricane season had finished at least a fortnight ago, nor was the swell of the long, oily type that presages a tropical storm, nor were the clouds of an ominous appearance. It was invigorating weather, that is all.

Ship's routine was again in full swing. At meals no one spoke to the Captain unless first addressed. Captain Edwardes was not privately a forbidding person, or even an impressive one; but his office was.

Captain Edwardes had not that naturally sovereign look which many sailors wear. He was a small man, rather cherubic, but dark. His eyes were bright, but it looked the brightness of excitement rather than of strength; and if his position had let him, one could see he would have been very affable. He was a native of Carmarthenshire: and for a Norfolk man, like Dick Watchett, it was anyhow difficult to revere a Welshman. The Chief Officer, on the other hand, Mr. Buxton, hailed from his own county: Dick would secretly have rather seen him in command.

Mr. Foster, too, the Second Officer—a solid, North-of-England man—he also looked a highly efficient seaman.

But an unprejudiced physiognomist, looking

21

round the saloon for someone on whom to place implicit reliance, would almost certainly have chosen the small, lean Devonian, the supernumerary Mr. Rabb, with his steady and brilliant blue eyes, and his firm jaw, his look rather of a naval officer than a mercantile one.

There was only one unpleasing thing about Mr. Rabb: his nails were always bitten right down to the quick.

It was two in the morning when they picked up the light on San Salvador. They left it ten or twelve miles to the eastward, passing between that island and Rum Cay, whose twin white cliffs just showed in the first of the morning light. They were now well among the islands, though keeping clear of all of them: the blue tower on Bird Rock was abeam soon after breakfast. The weather was still showery, with a moderate wind and swell: and for the rest of the day they sighted nothing, till they saw the tall tower on Castle Island at four in the afternoon.

Dick had never seen the West Indies before: it was disappointing to see now nothing of all those halcyon isles but an occasional light-house, or a low smudge on the sea, through rain.

At nine in the evening they were to the eastward of Cape Maysi, the easternmost extremity of Cuba, and entered into that broad channel between Cuba and Hayti which is known as the Windward Passage. The Cape itself lies too low to be seen in the darkness: but the dim tiers of the Purial mountains rose one behind the other against the lighter sky.

It was after five the next morning, and just getting light, when they passed to the east of Navassa Island; a barren limestone sponge, between Jamaica and Hayti. That was the last land they would see before they reached Colon, the entrance to the Panama Canal (where Mr. Rabb was to join his own ship). Ahead of them lay a short passage across the empty Caribbean sea—a passage of about forty-eight hours.

All that day it blew fresh from the north-east, and the black sea was rough. But what are a rough sea and half a gale to a fine modern vessel like the "Archimedes"? Enough to show her good qualities, not more: enough to prevent life on board her from being enervating. The wind whistled in the wires, and spray swept the foredeck, occasionally slapping some injudicious Chinaman as he tried to cross the well in his papery cotton clothes. It was enough to make Dick Watchett, on the bridge, feel himself a mariner; to blow away the lugubrious notion that a sailor's life nowadays was a process of cramming for examinations, and counting groceries.

Towards the evening it was blowing a whole gale. That was the maximum that one was likely to get, now the hurricane season was past. The seas were large enough to set "Archimedes" pitching and rolling; and if there had been passengers on board they would have lain mute and unsavoury in cabins, or half-frozen in deck chairs and lacking their usual good looks: or (a few of them) would have walked very fast up and down the deck, greeting each other heartily with hard grins, like diminished vikings. But there were no passengers on board the "Archimedes," not even pilgrims; and the only person who was sick was Thomas, and he did it decently and privately in the heart of the foghorn.

The reason for this wind was apparent when the wireless weather-report was received. A "tropical disturbance" was centred some hundreds of miles to the eastward: in other words, a circular system of gales round a central focus of low pressure, such as might, earlier in the year, have quickened to hurricane-force.

But the report described this one as of slight intensity and small area, and only shifting very slowly to the westward. In the records of the last fifty years, no hurricane of any magnitude has occurred in the month of November: the depressions always fill up and the wind dies away. And this was actually the middle of November. Nevertheless, caution being the watchword of the Sage Line, Captain Edwardes deflected his southerly course somewhat to the westward, to keep right out of its way. Not that a hurricane was remotely likely: not that a ship like "Archimedes" would care two hoots for a hurricane if it came. But however small the risk of danger, it is a navigator's duty to render it even smaller.

During this night the gale should blow itself out; and during the next night they were due in Colon. A slight rise in the barometer, which occurred late in the evening, proved conclusively that the gale must shortly be left behind.

But no: at six in the morning the barometer began to fall again, and the wind to blow really quite hard. To have continued trying to pass to the westward of the bad weather would no longer have been prudent, since there were reefs that way; and it is even more important to keep away from reefs than to keep away from winds. Colon was not very far off now, and the weather-reports from Colon offered gentle breezes and fine weather to anyone who would call and fetch them. So the new course set was south true, in order to get clear of the small area of disturbance in which it was quite plain they had somehow got involved.

At eight o'clock that morning Mr. Buxton decided to go round the ship, to tidy up and make all snug; just in case they were in for a bit of a dusting. It was a routine precaution, nothing else: one does not, in a vessel like the "Archimedes," adopt

the sort of measures—such as fixing hatch-pro-
tectors—one would adopt in a more vulnerable
little craft.

But he found that Mr. Rabb had been before
him, and had already made all snug off his own
bat. Nevertheless he went round himself too: not
that he did not trust Mr. Rabb, but the responsibility after all was his, as Chief Officer. He found
nothing to better: he could only admire the thor-
oughness and efficiency with which the job had
been done. "He's a good officer," he ruminated;
and then found himself adding, he hardly knew
why, "though a queer fish."

While Mr. Buxton was attending to the immediate situation, Captain Edwardes did some hard
and rather perplexed thinking. For it was now necessary for him to foresee, in accordance with certain meteorological rules, what the disturbance was
going to do.

The days of Conrad's *"Typhoon"* are passed:
the days when hurricanes pounced on shipping as
unexpectedly as a cat on mice. For one thing, the
mice know more than they used to know of the
cat's anatomy, of the rules which govern its motion
—and in addition to that, the cat has been belled.

By the turn of the century, meteorological science had already advanced a long way. The movements of these storms had been charted and studied over a long period, and their uniformity had

been found to be extraordinary. So every seaman was taught what paths West Indian hurricanes usually follow, and where the invisible obstacles lie which tend to deflect those paths towards the north. Thus he could generally avoid running into a hurricane altogether. But if he should find himself on the fringe of a disturbance, there were further rules which enabled him to calculate, by observing the barometer and the wind's change of direction, where the centre of the vortex lay at the moment; and so, whether he was in a quadrant where he would be sucked in, or buffeted out: in what direction to make his escape.

For, just as a rapidly-spinning top only creeps across the nursery floor, so, though the velocity of the hurricane wind itself is huge, the shifting of the whole system is not very fast. It seldom averages more than twelve miles an hour, while the storm is intense: and is sometimes only three or four.

And yet, sometimes ships used still to get caught. Some slow-moving sailing-vessel, or laden steamer: either an eccentricity of the storm's motion trapped her into a false move, or else she did not discover her danger quickly enough to get away. Now, however, with the advent of wireless, there is little danger even of that. For now, when a hurricane is abroad, all shipping in its neighbourhood keeps tag on it, and telegraphs data regarding it to a shore station. Thus, be its behaviour never so eccentric, the meteorologist on shore is able to watch, as plainly as with his direct eyes, every movement of the hurricane and every variation of its strength: and the least tendency to diverge from the path and the velocity forecast can be immediately observed: and the news, twice a day, can be broadcast back to shipping.

That is really what I mean by "belling the cat." You can hear the bell tinkle, twice a day. You can hear the hurricane's approach before it is anywhere near you.

It is usually fixed things, such as banana trees, one hears of nowadays as having been damaged by a hurricane: not shipping. Ships (which can run) are safer in those latitudes than government offices (which cannot).

III

The thing to remember about the atmosphere is its size. A little air is so thin, so fluid; in small amounts it can slip about so rapidly, that the conditions which give rise to a hurricane cannot be reproduced on a small scale. In trying to explain a hurricane, therefore, one must describe the large thing itself, not a model of it. For it is only when one thinks of the hugeness of a parcel of air on the world, the big distance it may have to shift to equalise some atmospheric difference, that one can realise how slow and immobile, regarded on a *large* scale, the air is.

It happens like this. The air above a warm patch of sea, somewhere near the Canaries, is warmed: so it will tend to be pushed up and replaced by the colder, weightier air around. In a warm room it would rise in a continuous gentle stream, and be replaced by a gentle draught under the door—no excitement. But on a large scale it cannot: that is what is different. It rises in a single lump, as if it were encased in a gigantic balloon—being actually encased in its own comparative sluggishness. Cold air rushes in underneath not as a gentle draught but as a great wind, owing to the bodily lifting of so great a bulk of air.

Air moving in from all round towards a central point: and in the middle, air rising: that is the beginning. Then two things happen. The turning of the earth* starts the system turning: not fast at first, but in a gentle spiral. And the warm air which has risen, saturated with moisture from the surface of the sea, cools. Cooling, high up there, its moisture spouts out of it in rain. Now, when the water in air condenses, it releases the energy

*The earth is a ball, turning about an axis: so a point on its surface near the Equator is moving faster than a point further from the Equator. The border of a system of air, therefore, which is nearest the Equator, will show a tendency to lag behind the border which is over a slower-moving part of the Earth's surface: and, if the system is limited, will give it a twist.

that held it there, just as truly as the explosion of petrol releases energy. Millions of horse-power up there loose. As in a petrol-motor, that energy is translated into motion: up rises the boundless balloon still higher, faster spins the vortex.

Thus the spin of the Earth is only the turn of the crank-handle which starts it: the hurricane itself is a vast motor, revolved by the energy generated by the condensation of water from the rising air.

And then consider this. Anything spinning fast enough tends to fly away from the centre—or at any rate, like a planet round the sun, reaches a state of balance where it cannot fly inwards. The wind soon spins round the centre of a hurricane so fast it can no longer fly into that centre, however vacuous it is. Mere motion has formed a hollow pipe, as impervious as if it were made of something solid.

That is why it is often calm at the centre of a hurricane: the wind actually cannot get in.

So this extraordinary engine, fifty miles or more wide, built of speed-hardened air, its vast power generated by the sun and by the shedding of rain, spins westward across the floor of the Atlantic, often for weeks together, its power mounting as it goes. It is only when its bottom at last touches dry land (or very cold air) that the throttle is closed; no more moist air can be sucked in, and in a few days, or weeks at most, it spreads and dies.

IV

But in November the conditions are seldom right, in those latitudes, for all the several stages of the forming of a true hurricane. The process occasionally starts: but then it dissipates, it dies, it becomes a mere "depression" (most depressions that reach England are really such dead or aborted hurricanes).

The first weather-reports evidently expected that this disturbance would be no exception. But the "Archimedes" had already left far behind the prognosticated path of the storm. Such storms, moreover, usually re-curve towards the right-hand, not the left. Yes, by every rule of the game they should be clear of all trouble by now.

But at nine o'clock on that November morning of 1929, the strength of the wind was found to be still increasing; so it was plain that something quite unusual was happening. First, this was developing into a true hurricane; and second, it was not at all where it was thought by the pundits to be. Either it had changed its course prodigiously, and in the wrong direction, or else—the notion flashed through Captain Edwardes's mind—this was not a single hurricane but a twin: he was being rapidly overtaken by a second and far more powerful vortex, not the recorded vortex at all.

He had told his chief officer, an hour before, that if the barometer continued to fall he should heave-to. The ship could thresh on, surely; but there was nothing to gain by subjecting it to such

31

únnecessary strain. Better point her nose into the wind, keep her engines running just hard enough to hold her there, and ride it out. For the process should not be long; a terrific gale for a few hours from one quarter; then a short time of calm while the centre passed over: and then the wind from the other quarter, gradually weakening as the storm left them behind.

At nine o'clock therefore, as the barometer still fell, and the steady direction of the wind showed that they were in the direct track of the storm, Captain Edwardes headed her round north-east and north, with her nose splitting the gale, to ride it out.

Chapter III

Dick Watchett was busy, and excited. This was his first hurricane; and he looked forward to it. Moreover the Captain—since captains are schoolmasters as well as everything else—made him in imagination commander of the ship; required him to repeat, from barometer and wind-direction, the same calculations that he had made himself, and say what should be done. It was interesting, but an ordeal (because the Captain's report on him at the end of the voyage would depend on the answers he made).

Once that was over, he was like a schoolboy out of school. He hoped that the hurricane would do something spectacular; that the wind would bend solid iron rails with its weight, something tangibly to express its force: something vivid, for letters home. But one could hardly hope for anything really spectacular on so large and well-found a ship as the "Archimedes." No dismasting. No frozen

33

helmsman lashed to the wheel, with salt spray glittering in his beard. No: for the strong wheel-house was up in the centre of the bridge, far above any waves, and thick panes of glass protected you completely from the weather. Nor was it a viking figure that stood at the wheel: it was a little old Chinese quartermaster, with a face like a wrinkled yellow apple, standing on a little old mat.

At eight, when Mr. Buxton had gone his rounds, he had taken Dick with him. Going about the deck, against this wind, was exactly like going up hill: the same effort, and the same slant of one's body towards the ground. The ship might just as well have been standing up on its stern, as facing the wind, when you tried to go forward: and coming aft was like falling downstairs.

The loud rustling shriek of the gale was giving place to a deafening roaring. The water sloshing about on the fo'c'sle head was atomised by the wind, and blew aft as mist. The water on the rails was blown off in little glittering fans. Even oil from the winches was carried by the spray to the upper deck.

And over the side one saw, not the familiar sea, but rather whole countrysides of water. The wind picked the skin off the waves, leaving little white pock-marks. Waves broke, and then swallowed their own foam: you could see it far below the surface, engulfed. Suddenly a squall of rain dashed across. The rain-drops bounced on the water, mak-

ing a surface like the dewy gossamer on a lawn:
like wool. It was as if the naked sea were growing
hair.

Instantly it was a great pleasure to Dick that
Sukie was not there. Wind was better than women.
A ship-load of men, none of them—at any rate for
the respite of the storm—in love with anyone: all
purely bent on the impending battle with the air.
That was best.

The thought of Sukie brought the taste of corn-
whiskey into his mind; and his mind repelled it
with vigour. He felt a sudden conviction that he
would never again touch alcohol: it was revolting
stuff. Not so much as a glass of beer. Nor smoke.
It surprised him a little; for he had always taken
a normal pleasure in these things. It was like conversion—a physical conversion, not a spiritual one,
for there was no morality nor resolution in it. It
was just a sudden reversal of his physical appe-
tites, so strong that he could not believe they would
ever change again. A loathing of girls, drink, tobacco; and all wrought by the wind.

Then the exultation which the storm had raised
in him whirled up in his head giddily, and he was
sea-sick.

II

At nine o'clock, when the ship was hove-to, the
wind-force had been only seven (on the Beaufort
scale): and the barometer stood at 29.58. By noon

35

In Hazard

the barometer had dropped to 29.38; and the wind-force was ten. That is a great wind: we don't often get it as strong as that in England, even when the weather seems to be blowing itself inside out: but it still continued to increase.

Plainly the storm was neither of the mildness, nor in the position, predicted. It was lucky that they had had all loose gear and so on secured in plenty of time. It would have been difficult now. It was difficult even to get about.

The seas, huge lumps of water with a point on top, ran about in all directions in a purposeful way at immense speeds. They were as big as houses, and moved as fast as trains. Sometimes they ran into each other, hard, and threw themselves jointly into the air. At others they banged suddenly against the ship, and burst out into a rapid plumage of spray that for a moment hid everything. The windows of the bridge, high up as they were, were completely obscured by spray: it was only through the little "clear-vision screen" (a fast-spinning wheel of glass which water cannot stick to) that it was possible to see at all. For if you stepped out on to the ends of the bridge, where there was no glass, the wind blew your eyes shut immediately.

Directly beneath the bridge were the deck-officers' quarters, a little room for each: and directly beneath that again, grouped just aft of the common dining-saloon, were the engineers' quarters. On each side there was a short corridor; and the

36

steering-rods from the bridge above ran along it. On to the starboard corridor Mr. MacDonald's room opened: on the port corridor the doctor lived.

This Dr. Frangcon was an elderly man, who never talked about his past. But a ship's doctor's is hardly a life for the professionally ambitious, and few elderly men are to be found in it. The only clue to his past (if it can be called a clue) was a package of medals which he kept hidden in a drawer among his underclothing. No one ever had got a good view of them: and while some said they were Boer War medals, others held that they were foreign decorations: but the steward maintained that they had been had for swimming. And Dr. Frangcon collected antique musical instruments— lutes, serpents, recorders and so on. These he brought to sea with him, sealed in glass cases to protect them against the changes of climate. He spent the morning anxiously wadding these glass cases apart with lint and surgical dressings, as the motion of the ship threatened to clap them together.

At two o'clock Mr. MacDonald, being rather old, went to his room for a rest: and Dick Watchett also went to his room, to see he had left nothing breakable in a place where it could break. The fourth engineer was left in charge of the hissing engine-room. Captain Edwardes and Mr. Buxton were both on the bridge, and intended to remain there. The wind was still increasing. The roaring so hammered on the ears as to tend to frighten the brain within. The atmosphere was almost all spray now: you could not see through it. Except for occasional momentary lulls, you could not see the sea, or the deck even. It was only by the wincing of the ship you knew what huge waves were hitting her: by that, and the thunderous banging. You could not *see* anything. Standing in the damp chartroom, you could descry, through the glass between, the little Chinaman, on his mat, at the wheel; but nothing outside: and it was only by shouting close into each other's ears that they could hear, either.

However, the fiercer a hurricane is, the smaller the area (as a rule) which it covers: and so the sooner it should be over. By that evening, with luck. That was, if nothing untoward happened.

But at two o'clock, there happened something very untoward indeed. For at two o'clock the engines, at half-speed, began to appear to be inadequate to keep her nose into the wind. So Captain Edwardes telegraphed for full speed ahead. Yet that seemed to make no difference: the propeller, unable any more to hold her, only roared in the helpless milk under her stern.

She was turning. The seas were battering more on the starboard side. The wind was on the starboard bow.

The quartermaster was making frantic signs,

through the window, that something had gone wrong with the steering. So that was it! However, there was nothing to be done but watch the compass-needle creep round in the compass. For by the time anyone could get the emergency wheel on the poop in action, she would be broadside; and then no power on earth could straighten her again till the wind eased. It took about five minutes, altogether; and then she was lying broadside on to the wind, heeled over steeply, vulnerable; and Mr. Buxton, noting the time, entered it in the log.

He also noted, with satisfaction, that her motion was a short, sharp rolling. This might be uncomfortable, but from the point of view of stability it was satisfactory. But she was heeled over so far that walls and floor seemed to have almost equal claims to represent the horizontal.

In the wheelhouse the little Chinese quartermaster clung to the useless wheel, like a cold monkey to the neck of its master. A sudden lurch tore him off. The mat on which he stood skiddered down the steep slope of the bridge: a snapshot (from the chartroom) of the Chinaman shooting by, with a concentrated expression, on his inadequate toboggan: then he fetched up against the rails at the far end with such a terrific impact as to bend them, and send the shield of the navigating light spinning into the sea. There he stopped, inert, on the brink: till Buxton and the Captain together managed to drag him back. Was he dead or alive? One does not bend iron rails with one's body for nothing. Yet, oddly enough, he was alive.

Gaston, the fourth engineer, a young dark Channel-islander, in temporary charge of the engine-room, telephoned for help. The engine-room sky-light had blown off, deluging the engine-room with spray, and fusing the lights; and with the ship heeled right over like that the engines would anyhow have been difficult to work. The second and third engineers came, but not Mr. MacDonald. For, leaving his room, he saw that the coir matting in the corridor had got jammed in the steering rods; and he was down on hands and knees, tearing at it with his finger-nails.

These steering-rods were his: and though the matting was Mr. Buxton's he knew he ought to have vetoed its presence in that passage, near his rods. But he had not noticed it: and now it had jammed the steering.

As soon as he felt the ship turn, Dick Watchett tried to leave his room. But he could not. The wind had fixed the door shut. It would have held it against an elephant. He was a prisoner there. He would have to stay there till a lull came and let him out.

Captain Edwardes telegraphed to the engine-room to reduce speed to dead slow: if full speed ahead could not hold her, it was better to save the engines.

The force of the wind continued to increase. Through its solid roar nothing—not even the impact of the seas—could now be heard. Captain Edwardes had been through several hurricanes; but never anything like this. He tried to assess its velocity: but he had nothing to go by. There is no figure on the Beaufort Scale to express such a wind-force as this was. No anemometer is made that would register so great a ferocity of air. Any anemometer yet made would be smashed by it. He thrust his hand out, for a moment, into the force of the spray, then drew it back bleeding at the finger-tips, and numbed as if by an electric shock. For the wind was blowing now with a velocity of about two hundred miles an hour. It begins to be called a hurricane when it reaches seventy-five; and the pressure at two hundred would be seven times greater. To be exposed to a wind like this was of the order of having to cling to the bare wings of an aeroplane racing.

When a hurricane blows the roof off a house, it does not as a rule get inside the house and burst it from within. The flow of the wind over the roof makes a vacuum on the lee side of the roof, and so sucks it off. When the "Archimedes" heeled over away from the weather, her deck made an angle very similar to the lee side of a roof: therefore the suction this wind exerted on it must have been terrific. But decks, of course, are enormously strong.

In Hazard

Hatches, on the other hand, are not. They are the most vulnerable part of a ship: and just as vulnerable on a big ship as a little one, because on almost every ship that ever sailed, from a liner to a coasting smack, they are made exactly the same. They are a set of oblong sections of wood, of standard size (each one no larger than can be conveniently shifted by two men), laid loosely upon beams, the whole secured by a covering of tarpaulin stretched tight and fastened round with wedges.

This system can resist immense forces applied from above; it can stand up to the pounding of hundreds of tons of sea. But pressure from below is a different matter—it is not designed for that. You do not expect there to be a vacuum created on deck.

Shortly after three o'clock, the wind, though it maintained its full force, and in gusts increased it, became more unsteady: thus there were rifts in the spray, through which an occasional view of the sea could be had. It was through one of these rifts Captain Edwardes saw some wreckage float by.

"Someone else is in trouble beside us," he said.

"They aren't," said Mr. Buxton, who was familiar with every inch of the ship. "Those are *our* Number 2 hatches."

III

The spray had cut the tarpaulins, as with a knife: and the wind had sucked the hatches out like drawing a cork from a bottle. Though no heavy seas were coming on board, the spray was so nearly solid water that hundreds of tons would find their way below in a very short time.

It was then Mr. Buxton recollected with foreboding how he had stowed the cargo. All those newspapers and that tobacco in the 'tween-decks— high up. All that water going below: it was bad enough if it cascaded to the ship's bottom, gradually filling her: but even if that happened, it would take a long time, and could be pumped out fast enough with the steam-pumps, and at least it would not affect her stability. But newspapers, and tobacco, are absorbent. Soaked with water, they would be many times their usual weight: and such a weight, high up, might conceivably turn her right over. He looked at the clinometer: her list was increasing, she was heeled at 35° and rolling to 40°. Those hatches ought to be covered again, somehow, at whatever risk; at least till the water could find its way right down.

IV

Dick's door remained jammed. He was shut in a little iron cube, tilted up on one of its edges, and jerking about like a rook's nest in a gale. Even without the motion, the thunderous yelling of the wind would alone have been intolerable.

He tried to get into bed, but could not stay there: the bed flung him out. He tried to lie on the

43

tilted floor, wedged against the wall: but even the floor flung him away; and small loose things fell on him: it was like being inside some joke-machine in an Amusement Park, worked by the Devil. The only way not to be flung about was to stand up, wedge his feet in two places and cling to something with both hands.

But Dick Watchett was not the only one who had been imprisoned in his cabin. The door of the midshipmen's room had also jammed. However, the same unsteadying of the wind which had revealed the floating hatches released them, though it did not release Dick: and the three boys burst out. Immediately they climbed to the bridge; though it was mad, going up stairs tilted on their sides, so that half your weight was on your elbow against the wall.

The sight of the three boys bursting suddenly on to the bridge gave a feeling of warm pleasure to Captain Edwardes; for he felt as if he had been there for ever, alone with Mr. Buxton; as if there was no one else in the ship. Now they came crowding up—the tall one, the fat one, and the thin, dark-eyed one—looking at him with implicit confidence: and that filled him full with vigour and pride.

Captain and Mate do not generally think apart, in urgent matters. The soaked tobacco and newspapers were as present in Edwardes's mind as Buxton's.

"Try and secure No. 2 hatch," he said. "Take everyone you can get.—Here, you Bennett" (to the dark thin boy), "stir out the seamen in the fo'c'sle, and take them along."

Buxton called the other boys to follow him, and struggled down the ladder: blind and deaf the moment he left the bridge, moving with as much difficulty as a weak baby.

But the boys were newly out of shelter. The blast blinded them and deafened them, even on the bridge. Bennett just heard the captain's order, and went about it: but the others neither heard the mate call them to follow him, nor even saw him go. They were filling up with air, as if their lungs were balloons being pumped; it made them feel giddy, and feckless—almost ready to giggle.

Buxton did not know that: he thought they were with him. It was all he could do to make his own way to the fore well-deck: those behind must look after themselves. Thus he was down there before he discovered he was alone. Never mind: Bennett and the Chinamen would be along soon.

Clinging in a doorway, he looked out. Mostly all he saw was shifting shafts and bars of spray— the course of the air grown solid and visible. Behind each obstacle showed something dark which looked like its shadow and was really its shelter, forming a hollow conical gap in the spray that outlined it in stream-line shapes: and where the wind rebounded against the plain opposition of something immovable, atomised spray fringed the edges like short fine hair. Yes, it was actually possible, by looking, to *see* the gaps in the air through which a man might insinuate his body, working his way towards the open hatch! Buxton, without waiting for help, put it to the test: climbing from shelter to shelter as a man on rock climbs from ledge to ledge. And, like a climber, he never thought of going back. In a minute or two he was there, crouched under the lee of the coaming; and as each volume of spray went below, he winced as if it fell on his own nerves.

A man on a good ledge or rock can belay and stay there: but Buxton's shelter under the coaming was not safety like that. He was protected from the wind; but the next sea which broke over the rail, as it might do any minute, would carry him away with it; for it would pour down this sloping deck like Niagara, there could be no hope of holding on. Even if he tied himself with a rope, the sea would batter him against iron things like an egg. And it might come any minute.

Nor was there anything to be done, even if he had not been alone. The hatches were gone clean overboard. To carry large planks, by however many willing hands, for repairing them, through the narrow spaces between the wind, was impossible. They would have to wait for the central lull—and meanwhile the stability of the ship must take its chance. He had better get back, before a wave caught him.

The hatches had gone overboard: but the tarpaulin, curiously, had not: it was pressed on the deck in a heap. Just as Buxton turned to creep away it leapt up, like a black wall. It hit him and knocked him down and covered him, flattening him to the deck under its stiff weight.

Then the sea came. It burst over the rail— God knows how many tons. It roared down the deck, a fathom deep: its weight nearly crushed Buxton, under the tarpaulin—the stiff tarred canvas suddenly fitting his body like a mould. Then away to leeward, over the other rail; and the ship staggered and rose. Buxton, under the tarpaulin, was not only saved alive; he was almost dry.

He crawled out, crushed and stupid, carelessly, so that the wind caught him. It was as if the climber on the cliff had slipped and fallen. The wind took him like gravity, and flung him to the centre-castle, where he crashed into the door from which he had started.

V

If nothing could be done on the fore-deck, still there were the after-hatches to consider. Some of them might have gone too. The after well-deck offered more shelter; so, if they had, it might be

47

just possible to work there—if he got enough men for the job.

Mr. Buxton went first to the saloon; where he found Mr. Rabb, his clear blue eyes staring straight in front of him, as if the worst storm could not affect his serenity. He was a comforting sight, to one direly in need of help. Mr. Buxton called him.

In the corridor he met the boy Bennett, with the Chinese bosun only, for none of the other Chinamen would come. They sat in a huddle on the fo'c'sle floor, he said: not attempting to hold on to anything, but sliding about as she rolled, bleating faintly as they bumped.

Then the tall boy, Phillips, appeared.

That made five. Five might do something. They made their way aft: and from the shelter of the centre-castle they saw what needed to be done.

No. 6 hatch was stripped also. But the planks had not gone overboard. If even some of them could be replaced, they could be lashed down, and the water going below could be checked. Nor was the position so exposed. It ought to be possible.

Indeed, Mr. Foster was out there already—busy with the stretching-screw of one of the mast-stays, which in spite of its locking-device was threatening to work loose. However, he was plainly too busy on his own job to be able to come and help them.

They had better make a dash for it.

They had better make a dash for it, at once. But

Mr. Buxton felt a curious unwillingness in his feet. All the top of him leant forward, but his feet seemed to creep backwards under him, like small rabbits looking for their holes.

This is not so bad as the foredeck, he said to himself; not half so bad. Safe as houses. "Come on!" he yelled, and flung himself forward.

Bennett and Phillips were after him like dogs off the leash. It never occured to *them* to be afraid, being new to it. They saw Mr. Buxton go, and they went: and landed on top of him, in a heap.

Buxton was out from under them in no time: beginning work before they knew which way up they were. One by one they got the hatches, dragging them up from the lee-scuppers. Then the mate and Phillips straddled the hatch-beams, the gaping hold under them, while Bennett worked from the deck. That was the hard part—*lifting* the hatches, without the wind getting under them. There was no sign of Mr. Rabb, nor the bosun. This was a big job for a man and two boys.

They got three in place, and lashed them. They were struggling with a fourth when a redoubled gust caught them. Mr. Buxton and Phillips clung under the beams they were straddling, like sloths. The hatch blew out of their hands, knocking poor young Bennett into the lee-scuppers, where he lay inert, washing about in the suds.

Mr. Buxton hoisted himself up, and was about

49

to go after him, when Bennett, revived by the slapping water, sat up. The first thing he saw was his leg: it was bent sideways at a right angle, just above the ankle. My God, he thought: I've bust my leg: it will begin to hurt, soon, a lot. Best get out of this before it begins. He moved gingerly— and it came right off.

Sitting there in the water, he blushed right round to his neck for being such an ass. Fancy thinking he had bust his leg! For it was only his sea-boot, of course, which had worked half-off as he skiddered, and then, being empty, had doubled up.

He made a grab at it, and then waited his chance to scramble back to the hatch-coaming.

Meanwhile, Mr. Buxton debated. His feet were bold enough now; but his heart was uncomfortable. By rights of course they ought to stick there till the last hatch was secured. But he did not want to kill the boys. They were regular little lions. It would be a shame if these boys were killed and all those bloody bleating Chinamen were not. It was the merest chance Bennett had not gone, that time. Anyway, they had stopped most of the water going down No. 6. "Come on," he yelled again: and all three made a dash for the poop. They crowded into the place where the steering-engine is housed.

It was lucky they did; for immediately the wind again began to blow with its greatest violence, and the open well-deck was impassable.

It is all very well while obeying orders with your whole strength; but sitting idle is different. Both boys, now they had leisure to notice, grew afraid, and thought the end was coming soon. The cold water in their clothes began slowly to explore their warm skins. No ship *could* stand it. Both inwardly began to say their prayers—each hoping the other would not guess. "The Lord is my Shepherd, I shall not want," said Bennett in the recesses of his head: "He shall feed me in green pastures, and lead me forth by the waters of comfort. Yea, though I walk through the valley of the Shadow of Death, I shall fear no evil: Thy rod and Thy staff shall comfort me." He did not know any more; so he began again, "The Lord is my Shepherd. . . ." It was childhood magic, used to fortify himself against the wild beasts of the dark, if he was sent upstairs alone. He had not used it since then.

But it was hard to keep his mind always on it now: and in between he would feel an agonising cold griping, in his stomach; a physical pang of regret. What a fool he had been to come to sea, when after all there was so much for him to do, in a long life, on the warm safe shore! All the infinite long years of childhood at last behind him; all to be wasted, no manhood to come after all.

Phillips, in a curious way, did not mind so much. He said the Lord's Prayer once, and left it at that. His mind divided into two halves. One half was actually glad. For young Phillips, for the first time, loved a girl with his whole soul; and she overlooked him. If he were drowned at sea, she would be told: his death would sadden her a little, even if his life was indifferent to her. There was no true living for him, he felt, except in her thoughts: then his death alone could secure him life, even life for the few minutes she would give to thinking of him. Like many young lovers, he confused a girl with God: and he could almost imagine her now, watching him, out of the sky; watching him die, and pitying him.

And yet there was another half of his mind, which was unshakenly confident. It was a part of his mind that did not argue, did not even put things in words; it knew things to be true; but it knew itself also to be under a taboo, that if it spoke those things, they would cease to be true. That part of his mind knew, now, that he was not going to die. It knew he was unique: mankind was divided into him on the one hand, and everyone else on the other. Death was for other people: *he* would not die, he would not ever die. God had made him different in this point—that he was not mortal, and was meant for a superhuman purpose.

Yet this confidence, because of the taboo, must never be put into words, even in his own head. He must let that other part of his mind run on, with its pathetic pictures of his tragic end, unchecked—as indeed it continued to do.

52

Wednesday

To this extent he was right, that he did not die that afternoon. None of them did. Instead they crouched there, unable to get out, in the faint stink of oil, for over two hours: till half past six.

VI

When Mr. Buxton and the boys made their dash for number 6 hatch, Mr. Rabb had wisely hung back: because he knew, even if he accompanied them, he would not have been much help, because he was too much afraid.

Fear often has the effect of making one over-exert oneself. If you are sent up aloft for the first time, and it frightens you, you will find yourself clinging on with every once of strength in your body, enough strength to hold up three men instead of one: this soon tires you, and leaves you no strength whatever to do what you were sent to do. If Mr. Rabb, afraid like that, had joined them at the hatches, he would have so grappled himself to the hatch-coaming as to be in a few minutes as weak as a new lamb with fatigue; and the first jolt would have shaken him off. There was no use in that. Only a wise man knows when he is too much afraid to take a risk successfully; just as only a wise man knows when he is too drunk to drive a car. But Mr. Rabb had had enough experience of fear, one time and another, to be able to look at himself when afraid clear-headedly from outside.

In Hazard

Obviously, now, the thing to do was to take no grave risks until he had got used to the situation, and his fear had melted away of itself—as it surely would do, in a short while.

He therefore decided to make his way to the bridge. That was a proper place, after all, for an officer to be in an emergency.

But perhaps he might stop for a rest somewhere, on the way.

Chapter IV

It was shortly before seven when Mr. Buxton got back to the bridge, the boys being still unable to leave the poop. Perhaps it was the best place for them, at present.

Mr. Foster was in there with them.

Captain Edwardes had been on the bridge all day: now the Mate was there to relieve him, he felt it was time to see personally how things were getting on elsewhere. The barometer had fallen to 26.99. So low a reading had never before been recorded for certain at sea. The dynamics of such a depression were beyond computation. Precedents, book-knowledge, experience—they were no longer a guide. The air might now be expected to perform feats no living sailor had had to face before.

Leaving the Mate in charge on deck, he made his way to the engine-room.

It was dark, the engineers doing their work by flash-lamps. The broken skylight had been barricaded, but spray still swept through it. The machinery groaned, all its bearings lying at unaccustomed angles. Chinese greasers, themselves greased, slipped about among it like muddy fish. On a little iron platform beside the telegraph the captain found Mr. MacDonald, his wise old face and grey moustaches dripping with oil and water. He was bitter with complaints: his machinery was not designed to work at an angle like that, and the skylight should have been battened down while it was still possible.

The second engineer, a red-haired Scotsman with a pasty white face, was on an everlasting round, reading steam-pressures and gauges of all kinds.

The third—a perky, opinionated little chap with the fixed expression of a frog, and the fourth (Gaston) were by the chief. They agreed it was doubtful how much longer engines, and men, could work under those conditions. For God's sake, couldn't the Deck do something about it?

"You're the only ones who can do anything about it," said the captain. "Your first duty is to keep up main steam. Well, keep up main steam and don't worry about the Deck. We must be near the centre now: in a few hours the worst will be over. That's not long to hold out. If you keep up steam we'll be all right—there's no damage done. Keep the pumps going in No. 2 hold and No. 6: then she'll right herself when the lull comes, and we can get her under control again and heave-to comfortable for the next blast. Fill No. 2 port ballast-tank—that'll help to right her. You can't steer and you can't pump without steam—so keep up main steam, whatever happens. It's not long now."

Well, the Deck knew. If the central lull might really be expected any minute, there was a chance of the engines holding out. Gaston, moving away to get the ballast-tank filled, was heartened. Nothing desperate had happened yet; and they were good engines. They had been working, in spite of the list, for over four hours without anything smashing. He peered into the stokehold: no trouble with the fires. The wind was not interfering with the funnel-draught seriously: at least, not more than the revolving fans, with their forced draught from below, could cope with. The fuel-pumps were working smoothly.

Only Mr. MacDonald was not heartened. He was old—contest had no call for him. Doubt meant foreboding, not excitement. He was old, and he liked certainty, reasonable conditions under which to render reasonable service. Moreover, an engineer comes to feel the stresses in big engines as if those engines were his body. To someone else the grinding of those bearings was a thing outside; but Mr. MacDonald ached with it, as if in his own joints.

Captain Edwardes, in spite of his tubby shape, swerved about these strange places with all a seaman's agility—that a seaman does not lose, at any age, till senility actually cripples him. He did not talk to the Chinese as he had talked to the officers; but they stole glances at him. He looked a very happy man: anyone could see, by looking at him, that everything was going all right. He entered the stokehold, and stood for a minute in the doorway, the light of the fires showing the immense secret pleasure in his face.

Then he left, to return on deck. It was as dark, by now, on deck, as it was below.

II

Coming out there into the blackness the blast hit him in the mouth, stopping his breath. He tried to gasp, but he could not: something pungent had filled his lungs, so that they retched and shuddered in the attempt to breathe. The wind was wrapping it round him in hot, greasy blasts. His unseeing eyes poured with water, smarted as in mustard-gas. He must be in a cloud of dense smoke: but he could not see it, of course—the night could be no darker than it was anyhow. He had no idea where it came from: possibly the fiddley. The thing to do now was to find his way to the Bridge—if his lungs held out. Keeping his head with an effort of will, he began to feel his way along, holding his breath (what little breath he had), resisting the dangerous temptation to hurry.

Down below, they had no more idea than the captain had, what had happened; though there too it was plain enough something was wrong. Just as he left, they heard a pop from the stokehold. A super-heat element had gone, thought Mr. Mac-Donald: nothing serious. But the next moment the firemen came out from the stokehold like bolted rabbits. Wisely, too: for steam was escaping, they said (steam at 200 lbs. pressure to the inch, heated to 600° Fahrenheit). No time to see where the leak was—only time to get out: for in thirty seconds the stokehold was uninhabitable.

Meanwhile, in the engine-room, you could see on the gauges the pressure of main steam dropping back, dropping back. What had gone? A mere super-heat element would not give an escape like that. Nor was there any way of finding out. A naked man can move without discomfort in air heated to temperatures above boiling-point, provided the air is perfectly dry, because the rapid evaporation of sweat keeps him cool. But if there is the slightest trace of moisture in the air, retarding that evaporation, it would kill him at once. Any considerable amount of steam would kill him at half the temperature of dry air. So imagine that stokehold, full of steam heated four hundred degrees above boiling-point! If you had ventured in, you would have been scalded to death at once; and then would probably have burst, after a few minutes.

Captain Edwardes found his way to the bridge, the smoke following him in eddies. Mr. Buxton was still there, of course. He had noticed the smoke; but could no more explain it than the captain could. Some trick of the wind, that blew it down on deck and perhaps . . . but that could hardly account for so much. They strained their eyes into the darkness till their eyes ached. But their eyes could not help them.

The roar of the storm was now so dense, so uniform, as to be the equivalent of a deep silence, in the way it wiped out all ordinary sound. You could not tell whether it was outside or inside you, like the pain in a deaf man's ears.

A message came up from the engine-room that something had gone: steam-pressure was dropping back.

As the pressure dropped back, of course, all the remaining apparatus that worked by steam began to fail. The pumps grew languid, stopped. The dynamos slowed down. The fans, which supplied the forced draught to the furnaces, stopped. When the fans stopped, the fires began to blow back, with explosions that burst open the furnace doors, and lit the inky engine-room with flashes of flame like lightning. The escaping steam had by this time cooled enough for it to be possible to enter parts at least of the stokehold: but the flames from the furnaces had taken its place as prevention. At each blow-back a tongue of fire thirty feet long would shoot out of the open fire-door.

Captain Edwardes now received a message that

main-steam had dropped to a point where the pumps had stopped, the fans had stopped, the dynamo was stopping: and the furnaces blowing back. It was eight o'clock.

But even if the fans had stopped, he considered, the funnel should at least give sufficient draught for the furnaces to function, though not efficiently. They ought not to be blowing back, just because the fans had stopped. Captain Edwardes and Mr. Buxton, through rifts in the spray, played electric torches on the smoke, trying to trace its origin. It must be coming from the *base* of the funnel.

It seemed to come from the base of the funnel, and must hide the whole length of the funnel within its cloud: for no funnel could be seen.

It was with a frightful sinking of the heart that Edwardes and Buxton together compelled themselves to believe what they were without doubt seeing. The smoke was rolling from a great oval hole in the boat-deck. The funnel was gone: must have gone overboard an hour before: yet such was the storm that Mr. Buxton, on the bridge, had neither seen nor heard it go!

Nor had it just crashed over the side: it had been lifted clear: for the life-boat to leeward of it was untouched.

That funnel, guyed to stand a lateral pressure of a hundred tons! A hurricane-wind, at 75 m.p.h., would exert a pressure on it of fifteen tons. But the pressure exerted by air (leaving humidity out of account) increases according to the square of its velocity: the pressure of a wind at 200 m.p.h. therefore, would be roughly seven times as great. And that would mean a total of . . . but you can work that out for yourself, as Captain Edwardes did, in his head, while Mr. Buxton ran into the engine room yelling "The funnel's gone! The funnel's gone!" like a maniac.

III

The steam-whistle-pipe was bracketed to the funnel: so when the funnel went, the whistle-pipe would go with it. Hence the escape of steam—from the broken pipe. That much was clear to every engineer the moment they heard the shocking news.

Now there was an emergency cock, for shutting off steam to the whistle: and there were two ways of getting at it. One was on the boat-deck, just to windward of where the funnel had been. But this one, being out of their province, they hardly gave a thought to; except to presume it was impossible to move on deck at all in these conditions. Looking back, one can at least say this: if they had drawn the captain's attention to it, a deck officer would have found some means of getting there: though he would likely have gone down the funnel-hole into the smoke-box, in the attempt, when another one would have tried his luck.

The other approach to this cock was on top of the boilers, close to the actual break.

This was the only one they thought about. But how to get to it? Being near the break, it would still be defended by hot steam. Nor, with the furnaces blowing back, could you get near the boilers at all.

An engineer's first duty (even without the captain's express orders) is to keep up main steam at all costs. But the furnaces were blowing back; and when they blew back, several of them altogether blew out, leaving hot oil squirting out of their nipples, running out of the fire-doors onto the stokehold floor. Mr. MacDonald's first instinct was that they must be re-lit. He and the Second were standing at the stokehold door, as close as they dared, when the furnace nearest to the door blew out like this.

"Heh, a torch!" yelled Mr. MacDonald: "Relight the aft-centre furnace!"

A Chinese fireman, dripping wet, slipped by them, drew the torch from its container, lit it at the next fire, and thrust it into the oven-like hollow of the extinguished furnace.

There was an explosion, blasting the furnace door clean off. For a moment the air was all flame, in which the only black thing was the Chinaman, in the heart of it, his arms up to guard his face. It licked both engineers, singeing their very skin. They heard the Chinaman screech. Then blackness; so black indeed that MacDonald and Soutar stood dazed, lights still flashing in their strained eyes.

In Hazard

Something was crawling between MacDonald's legs, coming out of that stokehold. He grabbed it, terrified—to find the fireman.

"Are you hurt?" cried Mr. MacDonald.

"My belong velly allight," said the Chinaman, quietly.

At that moment Mr. MacDonald found it was necessary for him to go to his room, to change his clothes: so he went, leaving Soutar in charge.

As soon as the chief was gone, Soutar called Gaston.

"We got to get at that leak, and turn off the cock," he said.

"Aye," said Gaston: "But we can't do it with the fires blowing like this."

"Then we must put them out," said Soutar: "put some of them out, so we can get to the boilers."

Now Gaston had noticed that the flames did not lick the floor: at their ends, they curled up instead. So Soutar and Gaston each took a broom handle, and lying flat on their faces they crawled into the stokehold—*beneath* the flames, like chops under a gas-grill. Then, reaching up with the broom handles, they contrived to turn off the fuel-cock of one furnace after another, their faces in the hot oil, their backs scorched with the flames. Thus they were able to get almost to the boilers. But one furnace defeated them. It was a double arrangement —two furnaces with a single combustion-chamber.

The after one they extinguished all right: but the forward one continued to blow back through it, and they could not get round to turn off the cock of that one too.

There was only one thing to be done: they must turn off the fuel-oil at the main supply. That meant extinguishing everything. Nor would it be easy, once the furnaces were cold, to light them again, with no funnel and no forced draught.

Not only would steam be gone—the fires would be out too.

Yet it seemed inevitable. Until the leak was checked, the fires could not raise steam, they were only a danger. The first thing was to check the leak. Once the escaping steam was turned off, the problem of re-lighting the furnaces could be re-considered.

The chief being away, Mr. Soutar, on his own responsibility, turned off the fuel, extinguishing everything. It was ten o'clock now: less than three hours after the captain's exhortation to keep up steam at all costs: and now the steam was gone, the fires were out.

By ten o'clock, then, the "Archimedes" was to-tally dead. Everything about her worked by steam or by electricity—so little, on a modern ship, is left to man-power. There being no steam, there was also no electricity. She was dark everywhere, but for the pin-points of a few electric torches and oil-lamps. Water still poured down her gaping fore-hatch—but the pumps were perforce idle. The wire-less apparatus, being dependent on main electricity, was dumb. Her propeller was still; her rudder im-movable. She was dead, as a log is dead, rolling in the sea; she was not a ship any more. She was full of men, of course; but there was no work for them to do, because ships having once discarded man's strength, cannot fall back on that strength in an emergency.

A well-found schooner of a mere two hundred tons, supposing she had weathered that storm, would not have been dead like that. Her pumps would have still been working, because they would have been worked by men: they could be worked as long as her crew lived. Her masts, of course, would have gone overboard; but once the storm relaxed, it would have needed mere carpentry to step spars against their stumps, rig jury-sails, re-pair the rudder, and so limp home. The very dis-tance a great modern steamer has advanced be-yond the little schooner is the measure of what a steamer's crew have to face, once her power has failed. Captain Edwardes, in charge of this lifeless log, in command of all these willing but unusable men, was well aware of that.

He found Mr. MacDonald in his room, still (aft-er half an hour) changing his clothes; and they returned to the engine room together.

Chapter V

At mid-night, Captain Edwardes went to the saloon.
A gimballed oil lamp was burning. The place was
a horrid mess. It was tilted steeply on one end,
and the lower end was awash; with splintered
chairs and smaller rubbish floating in it, and the
water slapping up occasionally to the higher end.
There deck-officers, boys, and a few engineers—
all mixed for once—had wedged themselves behind
a table, upright. No one would have thought of
sleep, even if it had been possible: they were waiting for the expected lull, now so long overdue. The
Chief Steward (a rotund, butler-like chap) was
with them. What little food—mostly biscuits—he
had in the pantry, he had locked up pending the
Captain's orders; for it would have to serve officers
and crew both, English and Chinese. The store-
room was flooded, he could not get out any more
till the pumps were working again. The only thing
he had plenty of in the pantry was spirits. But,

curiously, no one seemed to want any, not even a nip.

There was a smell of stale sea, stale food, and stale air: but there was another smell too: bitter, ammoniac. It was quite faint, but the Captain knew it. You do not forget it, if you have ever smelt it. It was the smell of fear. Disciplined men can control their muscles, even their facial expressions. But they cannot control the chemistry of their sweat-glands.

Captain Edwardes sniffed, and knew that the men needed some encouragement; so he gave it; his shaggy eyebrows sticking out like horns over his brilliant eyes, his tubby body planted like a light-house on a rock. For he felt himself full of power, like a prophet, with enough courage to serve out round the ship in ladles.

When the storm began, he had been worried: for this was not the first time he had run his ship into a tropical storm. Once before, when a young man, he had been caught in a typhoon, in his first command. It had not been a storm as fierce as this one, of course, and he had come through it without damage; but there is no need to get caught in typhoons nowadays, the text-books tell you: it is your own fault: and Owners believe the text-books. Moreover, what he had done that time had been deliberate: he had deliberately run into its expected path, though if he had stayed where he was the storm would have missed him. Yes; but where he was, that was an intricate net-work of channels and islands. There might be not one chance in ten that the storm would catch him, there: but if the tenth chance did catch him, with no room to move, his ship was as good as lost. On the other hand, if he put out to the open sea, it was nine chances out of ten the storm would catch him. Yes, but with plenty of room to move, there was no real danger if it did. He had argued like that; gone out: got caught in it, and came through safely. Still, it had been difficult to prove his policy to his Owners. In the end, they had forgiven him: but not forgotten. Owners do not forget. Or, if they do, they have only to consult their files to be reminded of everything.

So now that ill-luck had repeated history, and he was caught a second time, he might not be forgiven a second time. True, this time he had not flouted the text-books, he had done everything they recommend: and even then had got caught. Not a deliberate risk taken this time, just ill-luck. But he knew well that while a wise, deliberate risk may sometimes be forgiven, ill-luck is never forgiven.

Yes, he had been worried. But that was only at first. For soon the storm reached such a height that plainly this was no longer an issue between himself and his Owners, but become an issue between

69

himself and his Maker. That altered things. That suited him better. From then on, he was like an artist in a bout of inspiration.

The boys were the turning-point; when they came rushing up on to the bridge, courageous themselves, and confident in him. It was they who lit him. Then, later, as the storm increased to its immense height, so the flame brightened: his whole mind and body were possessed by intense excitement. No room for thought of his Owners. No room in him for anything but a gigantic exhilaration, and a consciousness that for the time-being all his abilities were heightened.

But back to the saloon. He was talking about the coming lull. "—shall need all hands then," he was saying. "There may be trouble with the Chinese. I rely on you gentlemen to put that right. You know, as well as I do, there's no danger to the ship if we all do our duty. By the afternoon it will all be over: be out in the sunshine. But the Chinese don't know that: they think they're going down. They're ignorant, and they got the wind-up. And when a Chinaman gets the wind-up he sits on his behind and don't do damn-all. It's up to you to show 'em, gentlemen. Let 'em see in your faces there's nothing to be afraid of. Then they'll do all you ask 'em. Cheerfulness. *You* know we're right as rain: well, let the Chinese see you know it."

70

Thursday

A few moments later he popped his head back into the saloon. "When the lull comes, all Deck-officers will report on the Bridge."

He had to roar all that, to make himself heard.

II

It was not till nearly two in the morning that the behaviour of the weather showed any change. Up till then, the wind had come upon them from the northeast almost in a single movement continuously. Now it grew fitful. It came from all sides, in blasts, as if big shells were being burst close about them. Gusts still very strong, but totally uncertain in direction.

Some of these gusts, coming up from what had been leeward with the lifting-force of an explosion, almost seemed as if they could blast the heeled ship back on to an even keel. But the weight of her sodden cargo held her implacably down: and other gusts, coming again out of the east and north, instead pinned her even lower.

Such an area of violent chaos, Edwardes knew, was commonly the torn fringe of the dead windlessness of a hurricane's centre. That centre must at last be near. It might not give a long respite: they must be ready for it. He whistled down to the saloon to call the officers. He sent Buxton on a tour of the Chinese quarters.

Buxton took his chance, in a dash across the

well-deck, to reach the "sailors' fo'c'sle." It was a single large room, with bunks all along one side and both ends, each bunk with a different coloured curtain (for Chinese seamen are particular about privacy). The whole room is usually very neat and clean: practically no smell: a Chinese calendar hanging on the bulkhead. But it looked different now. It was washed right out. No curtains, no bedding, no calendar: swirling water, and some burst straw mattresses floating: bare bunks.

No Chinamen there.

On the opposite side were the petty-officers' rooms. These, being meant for Europeans when the ship was built, were more comfortable than might seem necessary for the Chinese petty-officers that now used them (roughly, any specialist counts as a petty-officer: "idlers," they are called in sail). These too were deserted—except the carpenter's room. The carpenter was not there. But Mr. Rabb was.

He was standing, as if in meditation, holding on to the side of the bunk. Mr. Buxton told him to report on the Bridge: and he went without answering. Buxton wondered how long he had been there: it was a long time, he suddenly realised, since he had seen Mr. Rabb about anywhere.

Mr. Buxton made another dash across the well-deck, back to the centre-castle. It was there, in the two open spaces each side of the engine-room, that he found the Chinese seamen. They had gone hardly human. They were piled up, like a pile of half-dead fish on a quay. A lot of them were sick. With each lurch of the ship the pile spilt, or even skiddered entire against one bulkhead or the other; when the men in it showed they were alive by a faint bleat.

Mr. Buxton looked at them, appalled. How on earth would it be possible to get any useful work out of them? It was no good beginning to try to rouse them now. Wait till the lull came: they might feel better then. He returned to the Bridge.

III

All the other officers were already there, when he got there. Even Dr. Frangcon, and "Sparks," were there. Waiting. The lull should have come by now.

But by now, Buxton had begun to doubt if it ever would come. Many hurricanes are like that, he knew: no really calm centre at all, only a turmoil. They do not all do what the Air Ministry tells you.

Or again, perhaps the true centre was not going to pass directly over their ship. Perhaps it would pass a little to one side; this fringe would be all of it they would touch. He caught the Captain's eye: saw the Captain was thinking the same thing. Captain Edwardes, moreover, was doing some calculating in his head. They had taken a rather unusually long time to reach this centre—seventeen hours. It was quite on the cards it would take them another seventeen hours to come out on the far side. A lot of water can go down open hatches in that time. If as much went down as had gone already, she would capsize. The hatches *must* be repaired before the second bout.

"We'll begin right away," he said: "The wind's easing. Mr. Buxton will take charge of the fore-hatches, Mr. Rabb will take charge of the after-hatches. Mr. Watchett will go with Mr. Buxton. Mr. Foster, you see to getting the timber along: the engineers have it ready. Doctor, you stand by."

"If I were to speak to the Chinese, Sir, they know me better than the deck-officers," said Dr. Frangcon (which was true, for he had made a hobby of them in his search for strange music).

"Do what you can, Doctor."

Then, just as they turned to go, a terrific wave shivered the ship; tore the starboard gangway loose, so that it began to pound on the ship's side like a steam-hammer. Captain Edwardes crabbed his way to the bridge end, peering down with his torch to see what made the racket. He guessed what it was: but could guess no way to secure it. Luckily however the sea found its own way: after a few minutes it tore the gangway off altogether, and swallowed it, before it had time to batter a hole.

Then the Captain returned to the wheelhouse.

74

That place was a wreck. He flashed his torch round. The wind had not only smashed the windows, it had blown nearly every last chip of glass out of the frames, and now poured through the gaps. He had thought it deserted: but his light showed two men there, crouched down out of the wind-stream as if it were bullets.

Captain Edwardes flashed his torch again. They were Rabb, and Dick Watchett.

Dick, you know, had been shut in his room, unable to do anything except try to keep still, all day: ever since two in the afternoon, when the steering went. For the first hour he had thought about the ship going down: and claustrophobia clawed at him till he nearly went mad. He must find some way to banish it. He must compel himself to think hard about something else. At first therefore he tried to think about God: but God slipped about, and was shadowy. His home likewise: that slipped about, and cheated him. There was only one thing brilliant enough to hold his mental eye, during that time of strain: Sukie's body. He could hold that all right, he found. It was something brightly-lit and solid, among shadows.

Presently, though, his thinking turned to a queer quirk: for the image of her nakedness began to take hold of his body as well as his mind. He was sad about this, in a way; because he knew that he

75

could not love her as he believed he did, if he could think about her like that. Yet he deliberately continued. For his plight was *so* desperate: it was worth even spoiling his love, to keep himself sane.

But at last one of the huge buffets, when the wind unsteadied after mid-night, released the jamming of his door, and he got out. The prolonged effort of imagination had left him weakened: and with an added cause for fear, in that he felt God could hardly favour him now. He went straight from his room to the saloon, without going on deck: and stayed there with the others, till the order came for them all to report on the Bridge.

Thus his arrival on the Bridge had been his first contact with what the air was really doing now: he had not come to it gradually, as the others had.

Even then he was all right up to the very last minute, when the Captain gave his orders; he was on the very point of following Mr. Buxton down the companion when that terrific thud, which tore loose the gangway, flung him suddenly on his hands and knees. The next thing happened in a moment: instead of crawling down the companion after the others he found he had, almost without knowing it, crawled into the wheelhouse to hide.

He certainly did not know that Mr. Rabb had done the same.

As for Mr. Rabb, he had gone straight there

from the Chinese carpenter's room. He was not really conscious any more. His actions were automatic as a sleep-walker's, with the unswerving tenacity of purpose of pure instinct—like a shark snapping. He had been like that almost continously, ever since he first gave in to his fear over the first attempt to mend the hatches.

Now he crouched down in a corner, his face immobile, his eyes shut: while Thomas, with the absorption of a handicraftsman, his own nocturnal eyes glowing like lamps in the light of the torch, was endeavouring to pick those clamped eye-lids open again in vain.

Captain Edwardes cuffed the little lemur away, as you would drive a vulture off a dead body. Then he paused a few seconds to conserve his strange new energy, which now must be used to re-inflate these two collapsed figures.

"Mr. Rabb," he roared quietly: "Go aft and secure No. 6 hatch. Mr. Watchett, go forward and secure No. 2 with Mr. Buxton."

Mr. Rabb neither spoke nor moved; he did not seem to hear. But Mr. Watchett spoke.

"I can't, Sir," he said miserably.

"I don't give orders that can't be carried out, boy!" the Captain roared again, just as quietly. "You've got the wind-up, just for a moment. It'll pass. It'll pass, boy. Look, I'm going to count ten. When I say ten, you'll be all right. When I say ten, you stand up on your two legs. Diawl! I know you're all right, or I wouldn't waste time on you. One, two, three . . ."

As he counted, he kept his torch on the faces of the two of them. Watchett looked at Rabb: and saw for the first time what Fear looks like: its bare aspect. Watchett was deadly afraid of the wind: but fear like Rabb's, he saw, was something to be more afraid of than any wind. The clutches of the wind were the more tender.

"—Eight, nine. . ."

"Secure No. 2 with Mr. Buxton," he repeated mechanically, and began to crawl on his belly, feet first, down the companion, gaining heart as he went.

But Rabb did not move: did not seem conscious. Must be woken.

"You bloody skunk!" Captain Edwardes began; and did not stop at that. He kicked the man, and cursed on: ashamed of his language, for he was not a man used to cursing: but clinging desperately to his belief in its tonic qualities. He called back to mind words he had not used since he was a schoolboy. But the green, almost luminous wet stare of Rabb's face was his only answer. For all their effect, the words he used might have been mother's milk.

But he could not leave him like that. Fear like that is worse than plague on board: it spreads quicker. You cannot allow it.

Down in his cabin was his revolver. He turned to fetch it; for shooting seemed the only thing left.

Then he had another, a more intelligent, idea, as a thud huger than most shook the bridge. He let out a great simulated screech, and fell on the deck beside Rabb, clutching at him. "My God!" he cried: "Did you feel that? The bridge is going! The next bloody great sea'll carry away the whole bloody bridge, and every bloody man on it! For Christ's sake, man, let's get below while there's still time!"

A tremor ran through Rabb's body. Without a sound, without a flicker of expression on his dead face, he wormed his way to the top of the companion and disappeared. But Edwardes was with him. And when Rabb next came anywhere near to normal consciousness, he found himself sitting in a doorway of the centre-castle, superintending (after a fashion) old Dr. Frangcon and three Chinamen fixing new hatches over Number 6 hatchway.

When Dick Watchett got to the foredeck, he ran into Mr. Buxton in the dark. Buxton felt him shaking.

"What's the matter, Dick?" asked the Mate.

"I'm frightened," said Dick: astonished at his own shamelessness in confessing.

But Mr. Buxton did not seem shocked. "Of course you are. So am I. But you're *here*, that's all that matters."

In Hazard

On his way back to the bridge, Captain Edwardes stumbled over another figure, slumped in a corner. It was the boy Bennett: who had nearly been killed trying to fix the hatches the afternoon before. Now fear had got him too.

Edwardes did not try to encourage him. He picked him up and carried him into his own cabin: tucked him up in the bunk.

Chapter VI

That chaotic gustiness, with no sign of abatement, continued for half an hour. You could hear each gust coming by its distant howling, which rose crescendo till it hit you: sometimes, from different directions, two or three at once. They soon guessed it was all the "calm" they were to have.

It was utter black dark.

Yet the work was done—*hard*. Buxton and Dick, torches strapped to their waists, worked alone on the forward hatches, with Foster the second mate superintending supplies. Aft, Dr. Frangcon: who, by a miracle, had three Chinamen more or less composed and working with him. But they did not make much progress; for Dr. Frangcon was an old man, he had not the strength nor the practice for this job, though he had the heart. Captain Edwardes, shadowing Mr. Rabb, came down to take a hand himself; but that did not turn out well, because of the Chinese. They found it too much of an honour to work side by side with their captain, it turned them at once from seamen into flunkeys: so that the moment Captain laid hold of anything to pull or push, six yellow hands dropped whatever useful thing they were doing to pull or push for him. When he tried to work they took his work from him: and chaos was even worse.

So he gave it up. He went forward to take Buxton's place on the fore-hatches, and sent Buxton (being a shade less august) aft.

Buxton fell over Rabb, sitting in the doorway.

"You go forward now, Mr. Rabb," he said, "and help the Captain on No. 2."

Rabb blazed up in anger:

"Why pick on me?" he said. "This isn't my ship! You've got a down on me, you give me all the work to do. Can't I have a moment's peace?"

Rabb was truly furious. Here! He had been working all the day, and night, superhumanly, and always chivvied by the Mate! However, he turned to go: and really meant to go forward, only on the way those stinking black clouds began coming up again over his brain—fear had got him again. So he thought he would take a short rest first, and climbed down a companion; and found himself among the Chinese. Like blind puppies huddling together from the cold. Rabb paused for a moment near them: his fear was re-inforced by their communion of fear, and he began burrowing under them as if to disappear altogether from view.

II

Once the hatches were secured, Captain Edwardes sought out the steward to see if he could serve a meal. It was only then the Captain learnt there was next to no food to be had, and no water at all. So he and the steward divided out what there was among every man on the ship and served it by the light of the saloon lamp. It was a small breakfast, to follow seventeen hours' fast: just a biscuit or two each, and a tiny portion of Dutch cheese. The English put a good face on it at once: but the Chinese looked morose, and then went away and got money and offered it secretly to the Mate for extra rations. He could not convince them that there really was no more food to be had, for anyone; that everyone had shared alike. They were so sure that he and the Captain must have kept back a store for themselves, a little of which they might be prepared to part with for a dollar or two.

But the shortage of drinking-water was even more serious than the shortage of food. The tanks, I told you, were accessible through man-holes in the engine-room floor. But the engine-room floor was sloshing about with sea-water: to open a tank would simply be to spoil whatever was in it.

Only one of the freshwater tanks had its man-lid in a position where it could be protected from flooding: and that one, as luck would have it, was empty. Or rather, it was technically empty: as empty as the pumps had been able to make it. But the pumps are bound to leave a few inches at the bottom. So Gaston and the steward unscrewed the man-lid, and Gaston was lowered inside with jugs and dippers, and scooped up what he could. It was not much, but it gave them a small wet each; and that would have to last them till they were out of the storm, there was no more to be had. Then, before they replaced the man-lid, they let the flood-water run in, for ballast.

It was while this was going on that the ship passed out of the centre—if centre it could be called. The second round of the contest had been begun. Or so everyone thought.

When you pass towards the centre of a hurricane, the wind is (in the main) blowing one way. You cross it, and come out the other side: and there, of course, the wind is blowing the opposite way. As the "Archimedes" came out of the centre, the wind became once more fairly steady in one quarter. But it seemed to be still blowing in the same direction as before.

Had the ship turned round? Edwardes looked at the compass: no, she was heading much as she had been.

The "Archimedes," then, had *not* crossed the centre: she could not have. She had approached the centre, and then slipped back. She was back again in the same quadrant of the storm as before.

So the storm was not passing over them: it was sucking the "Archimedes" along with it!

84

Thursday

, Seventeen hours had once seemed a long time to have to wait for escape. Now it suddenly dwindled to a short, to a most desirable time. For Captain Edwardes now realised that it was impossible to count on escape even in seventeen hours: to count on escape at all, so long as the sucking strength of the storm continued. It was impossible any longer to count on anything at all.

With dawn it grew light; but things did not become visible. Spray—atomised ocean—hid everything. It was a white night, now, instead of a black one: that was all.

No one had slept; but only one man, through the early hours, had continued at work. That was Sparks.

Not only was his aerial carried away: he had plenty of other troubles. His main electricity, like everyone else's, was cut off. But there is an emergency paraffin-actuated generating engine provided, on top of the House, for just such a contingency. Yes: but at that moment a loose derrick, on top of the House, was busy pounding the emergency paraffin-actuated generating engine to pieces. Well then: there are emergency batteries, worth fifty hours continuous use, inside the House itself. Yes: but the scuppers of the House were choked, and the House was full of salt water: and when he had retrieved them, and examined them, he found that the emergency batteries, worth fifty hours continuous use, were full of salt water also. So to begin with he spent six hours drying out the batteries, with a blow-lamp. Then he had to set about drying out all essential parts of the wireless-room, by the same means, before he could hope to get the Emergency Transmitting Set to work, with an Emergency Aerial.

Nevertheless, by nine in the morning he succeeded. The beautiful big valve lit up, the motor whirred.

From fifteen to eighteen minutes past each hour there is a gap reserved, in ships' wireless transmission: a gap during which only signals of distress may be sent out. By nine-sixteen, Sparks had succeeded in ringing the auto-alarm in another vessel fifty or sixty miles away: was in touch with her: was hearing about *her* weather. She was experiencing strong winds: almost strong enough to make her believe (if this had not been November) that there might be a hurricane about somewhere—up to the north-east. So then the "Archimedes" told her there really was a hurricane about: but not up to the north-east of her, down to the south-west.

"Cannot understand your weather" she wirelessed back, a trifle huffily: and before the "Archimedes" could reply again the emergency set gave out. For the wireless room was once again drenched with salt water, and everything shorting.

That was at nine-thirty. Well, at least the outside world now knew that they were in trouble: the world outside the hurricane knew that there was a hurricane. The Owners, away in Bristol, would hear about it very soon. And would be very worried. It was a pity Edwardes could not get a message through to re-assure them, to tell them how nicely the "Archimedes" was doing, really. But there was no hope of getting the wireless going again, not while all this drenching spray lasted. They were cut off, and must fend entirely for themselves (and leave the Owners uncomforted).

But the mere fact of having communicated with another ship lent them heart. The hatches they had so painfully secured had by now blown out again. What of it? Their work had stood for at least a couple of hours. Two hours less of spray had gone below. Capsizing was two hours further removed—and that might make a difference. After all, if they came near the centre again they could mend them again; and so save another two hours, perhaps.

III

No one had thought about the engines much, once the fires were out: but now they began to think of them. Steam. The leak was stopped now: if they had steam again to work the pumps they could snap their fingers at spray going down the hatches. They must get steam up again somehow: So the Deck thought.

Captain Edwardes told Mr. MacDonald to re-light the furnaces.

In Hazard

It is not too easy a job, lighting the furnaces from cold: even in dock, with your funnel standing. The oil has to be pre-heated with blow-lamps —and that takes some time. Secondly, it has to be hand-pumped through the sprays, under pressure. Then, until you have steam enough to work the fans, you have to rely on funnel-draught alone. Now, with no funnel at all, the engine-room knew it could not be done. But the Captain was adamant: they must re-light the furnaces: and Mr. Mac-Donald passed on the order as if it was the easiest thing in the world to do: and the engineers set about doing it, just as if it was possible. It was not for them to tell the Chief it could not be done: he knew as well as they did. It was not for him to tell the Captain it could not be done: that was for the furnaces themselves. *They* would soon tell him, plainly enough.

As for the engine-room Chinese, for some reason they had not gone into a panic like the Chinese seamen. They felt it a grievance, that the Mate was apparently standing out for a higher price than they could afford, before disgorging any of his private food-supply: but that only confirmed them in allegiance to their own officers. Mr. Mac-Donald, they felt sure, would have been content with a reasonable profit, proportioned to their means. If the need came, in the future (if the Mate remained too avaricious) they would mutiny for

88

food: but it had not come to that yet: and in the meanwhile they obeyed orders just as if everything was normal. Gaston told them to light the blow-lamps that pre-heated the oil, preparatory to firing the furnaces. Did *they* know the task would be impossible? Heaven knows. They showed no opinion either way, they just set about lighting the blow-lamps. Working in the dark, heeled over and rolling, the engine-room floor under them flooded with a little stinking tide that rose and fell with every roll.

Heating the oil took several hours. Then at last the Chief gave the order to fire one of the furnaces. It blew back, as everyone knew it would —exploded. He sent up a message for the Captain to come: and the Captain came. No one spoke. They left it to that furnace to tell him, lighting and re-lighting it again and again for his benefit, until hot oil ran out onto the engine-room floor.

IV

Mr. MacDonald had changed his clothes, now, for good: he was fully on duty again. The old adapt themselves more slowly to things than younger men: but all the same, they do adapt. Mr. Mac-Donald's great experience, his obstinacy, and above all the almost physical way in which he was wedded to his engines, now propelled him into the fight against the storm with an increasing momentum.

In Hazard

A psychological momentum so great that henceforth, if he did get a chance to relax, to rest, he would not be able.

The Captain left them, and MacDonald turned to Soutar. "Donkey-boiler," he said.

The donkey-boiler is a small auxiliary, used for raising steam for small jobs (winches and the like) in harbour, that do not make it worth while to fire the main boilers. The donkey is housed in a little room by itself, above the engine-room, near the fiddley. It has its own funnel—a mere stove-pipe when compared with the main funnel, to which it is bracketed for strength. Being so bracketed, it had of course been carried away with the main stack. But nevertheless a few feet had been left standing. Moreover the donkey-furnace is a natural-draught furnace, it does not depend on fans: and that single section of its funnel left standing *might* be enough for it to burn.

So when Soutar called the other engineers off the main furnaces and told them to fire the donkey-boiler, they jumped to it. That was something conceivably possible. If it could be done—why, there was steam for the pumps at any rate. Perhaps even steam for the fans: and with the fans going the main furnaces might burn, funnel or no funnel. The ship would be alive again. Gaston was tired as a dog, but he set to work hand-pumping fuel (to get sufficient pressure for it to vaporise as it passed through the spray-nozzle) as if it had

90

been a light sport. He pumped like someone row-
ing for Oxford or Cambridge—and yet as though
he would gladly keep it up all day, if need be.
The Chief had not told the Captain what he was
about: the Engine-room was working on its own,
now, preparing a birthday-present for the Deck.

It was four o'clock in the afternoon when the
boiler was ready for firing. The blow-lamps had
done their work. Gaston had his pressure. The
Chief gave the word: the fuel-cock was opened:
a torch thrust into the corrugated antrum of the
furnace.

Well, at first it blew back like the main furnaces
had done. But they did not give up. Just a bad fluke
of the wind perhaps: give it a chance. A few explosions might be to the good, if they warmed
things up: might help to start the draught.

It may be that one of these explosions damaged
the spray-nipples. The hole through these is not
straight: there is a screw down the middle, so that
the oil is forced to race round and round its thread,
faster and faster as it approaches the aperture, ac-
quiring turbulence. Perhaps that broke. Or perhaps
some impurity escaped the hot-filter, and clogged
the passage. Or perhaps it was just insufficient
draught. Anyhow, the jets ceased to work. Instead
of coming out vaporised (or more strictly, pulver-
ised) the oil was dribbling through, liquid. Though
hot enough, all the same, to burn.

Even then, they were too keen to stop. Hot oil

was running out of the furnace doors, onto the donkey-room floor: but still they kept on. At first they hardly noticed, when that spilt oil caught fire. So in a few minutes the whole place was flooded with liquid fire, in which the engineers (luckily too wet themselves to ignite, for the moment) were caught plunging, as if they were playing a kind of beastly snap-dragon.

As she rolled, the fire crept up the iron walls; was sloshed up them, like water, and over the raised door-sill. And more oil was still running out of the nipples. If the fire spread beyond that room— well, the Deck would get their surprise birthday-present all right! Before long, in that confined space, in that growing heat, oil and air would form an explosive mixture. A sort of paralytic lassitude took Gaston for the moment. What was the use? That would end it quickly. What was the use, of continuing to fight when each new attempt at safety only added a new danger?

But the Chief, on the other hand, had men running to fetch fire-extinguishers like lightning: and Gaston's lassitude went. They joined together to fight the fire quite steadily, trying to smother it in the patent "foam." But still more oil came to feed it. It was growing on them, it was creeping up the walls: it would be over that door-sill for good, in a minute. But they worked methodically, not just at random: cutting up the fire into small areas: clipping round their edges: finally driving each separate flame into a corner and there smoth ering it, one after another. In the end, they won.

Gaston, wielding a foam-nozzle, happened to look round and see the Captain there, in the door-way, watching them. Well, now the Deck knew. There was *nothing* else the Engine-room could do. From now on, it was up to the Deck—if anyone.

"All right," said Captain Edwardes, "Come out on deck. Repairing hatches again. We're in the centre now, good and proper."

The last flame had been extinguished: and as he spoke the engineers woke up to the outside world, that they had wholly forgotten in the blaz-ing donkey-room. They suddenly noticed that the roar of the storm was gone: replaced by a blanket-ing quiet. Yet something was wrong with the quiet: they still had to shout, to make each other hear, just as they had during the roaring. It was as if the quiet was indeed a blanket: not just an absence of sound, but able to smother sound: a thick, soft thing. Something that smothered their voices in their throats, padded their footfalls.

They did not realise that you cannot live in such a din as they, for a long while, had lived in, without being deafened.

The air was gaspingly thin, as on a mountain: but not enlivening: on the contrary, it was damp and depressing; and almost unbearably hot, even

93

to engineers. Big drops of sweat, unable in that humid air to evaporate, ran warm and salt across their lips.

The tormented black sky was one incessant flicker of lightning.

For the first time, since the storm reached its height, they could see the ship from one end to the other. For the first time they saw the gaping crater left by the funnel's roots. Smashed derricks, knotted stays. The wheelhouse, like a smashed conservatory. The list, too, of the ship: that had been at first a thing felt: then, as they grew accustomed to it, almost a thing forgotten; but now you could see the horizon tilted sideways, the whole ocean tipped up at a steep slope as if about to pour over the edge of the world: so steep that it seemed to tower over the lee bulwarks. It was full of sharks, too, which looked at you on your own level—or almost, it seemed, from above you. It looked as if any moment they might slide down the steep green water and land on the deck right on top of you. They were plainly waiting for something: and waiting with great impatience.

But the sharks were not the only living things. The whole ruin of the deck and upper-structures was covered with living things. Living, but not moving. Birds, and even butterflies and big flying grasshoppers. The tormented black sky was one incessant flicker of lightning, and from every masthead and derrick-point streamed a bright discharge, like electric hair; but large black birds sat right amongst it, unmoving. High up, three john crows sat on the standard compass. A big bird like a crane, looking as if its wings were too big for it when folded up, sat on a life-boat, staring through them moonily. Some herons even tried to settle on the lee bulwarks, that were mostly awash; and were picked liked fruit by the sharks. And birds like swallows: massed as if for migration. They were massed like that on every stay and handrail. But not for migration. As you gripped a handrail to steady yourself they never moved; you had to brush them off; when they just fell.

The decks were covered in a black and sticky oil, that had belched out of the funnel. Birds were stuck in it, like flies on a flypaper. The officers were barefoot, and as they walked they kept stepping on live birds—they could not help it. I don't want to dwell on this, but I must tell you what things were like, and be done with it. You would feel the delicate skeleton scrunch under your feet: but you could not help it, and the gummed feathers hardly even fluttered.

No bird, even crushed, or half-crushed, cried.

Respite? This calm was a more unnerving thing even than the storm. More birds were coming every minute. Big birds, of the heron type, arrived in such numbers, that Captain Edwardes, in his mind's eye (now growing half delirious), imagined the additional weight on the superstructure actually increasing the list: them arriving in countless crowds, and settling, and at length with the leverage of their innumerable weights turning the "Archimedes" right over, and everybody sliding down the slippery decks to the impatient sharks. Little birds—some of them humming-birds—kept settling on the Captain's head and shoulders and outstretched arm, would not be shaken off, their wings buzzing, clinging with their little pinlike toes even to his ears.

Only work could take your mind off the birds; and luckily there was plenty to do, fitting new hatches and covering them with awnings for tarpaulins: but how could even work take your mind off, with birds settling on you and clinging to you even as you worked?

They longed for the wind again: but the work was finished before it came.

When at last the blast came, from an opposite quadrant, sweeping all those birds away to destruction, everyone was heartily thankful. Thank God not one of them was ever seen again.

Part II

Chapter VII

At noon the next day the Captain and Mr. Buxton were on the Bridge together. That was Friday: they had been in the hurricane since Wednesday morning. Early Thursday morning, wasn't it, they had something to eat—those biscuits? And a little water? As for sleep, they had not had any for two nights; nor even any rest.

The storm was blowing full pelt again: had been, ever since the birds went.

The lack of sleep gave a sort of twinge occasionally in the Captain's brain: as if someone with fine tweezers was plucking at his consciousness, tweaking out a split second every now and then. If this got worse, he was afraid he might reel and fall: and anyhow, each twinge left him feeling a little sick. Buxton must be feeling just as bad. So he turned to Buxton:

"You'd better get a bit of rest."

Buxton went into the wheelhouse, wedged his feet against the binnacle and his back against the bulkhead; held onto the nerveless wheel and let his head fall forward on his chest.

Ten minutes later Buxton woke, to see a wave towering right over him like a tree. He was already out of the wheelhouse, and running down to the deck: yelling to them to get their life-belts on, for the ship was going.

Those who in the everlasting noise could not hear him, could see what he meant.

The boys saw him cutting his trouser-legs off short at the knee, so as to be able to swim better, so they did the same.

The sea was awful: worse than it had ever been. You could see this was not deep water: free-bottomed waves do not rear so wildly (for a wave is not a thing with a top but no bottom, as you would think by looking at it: the shape and forces of a wave are just as much under as above: and if a wave is hampered beneath, on top it must burst).

Captain Edwardes ordered the lead to be cast: and it was cast, but the wind blew it out across the water nearly level. Sixty fathoms, it read. But that was nonsense: this was not sixty-fathom water. They were over a bank. Where? He could only guess. Might be Serrana: might be Serranilla: anyhow, how could you tell what the normal level of the water was here? Near the centre of such a vortex, the ocean would be drawn up in a great pucker, with them on top of it. Why, this might even be normally dry land; a cay or island; and

100

they, sailing over without bumping, complaining because it was broken water!

These waves really had the size and almost the shape of trees—trees galloping about, lashing and thrashing each other to bits, like that game of Kings and Queens which children play with plantains.

A few such waves, falling on deck with the hatches open again would soon fill her up, and down she would sink. Go on! Cut off your trouser-legs; and put on your life-belts! Then let us see you do your fancy swimming-strokes among these waves! Waves that will drop on you from seventy feet above you, weighing five hundred tons a time! And where do you think you will swim to, in the Name of Christ?

One wave already had come down on the deck, like a really vast oak crashing. A *few* more would sink the ship.

Then came another great wave that landed right on top of the funnel-hole. It must have been still hot down there, for that wave came out again faster than it went in: spouted out again roaring and black with soot. When they saw the steam and soot people started yelling *Fire!* When he heard them yelling *Fire!* MacDonald thought some fool had been trying the donkey again, and really done the damage this time. When he heard them yelling *Fire!* Buxton thought of the drums of alcohol stored in the after-castle; the only badly inflammable cargo

101

they carried, now everything was sodden . . . but what nonsense, alcohol would not burn with a lot of smoke and black soot, it would roar sky high with the first spark. What a fool, to think alcohol might burn like that!

I must be losing my head.

So then he began paying attention to that most important thing of all, not losing his head: and in no time was clear cold sober again. He looked at the towering waves, and at his own foolish sawn-off trouser-legs, his silly life-belt: and felt his ears burning red.

That is what comes of going to sleep, he thought.

Oil was the only thing: and quickly.

There were latrines both ends of the ship: forward, latrines for the firemen and the seamen: aft, latrines for the pilgrims—male to port, female to starboard. Ships ought to have special arrangements for hand-pumping oil onto troubled waters: but they have not, and latrines are the next best thing. The only trouble with latrines is the baffle on the outside, which stops the oil from dropping really clear of the ship.

There was a reserve tank of lubricating oil in the top of the engine-room, up by the door. Captain Edwardes had it broached, for it was in a convenient position: the Chinese engine-room staff filled five-gallon drums from it, and trundled them as far as the well-decks, fore and aft. They would not go out into the open: so the deck-officers took over from there.

Watchett was sent to take charge of the forward latrine.

Just then the boy Bennett appeared again, out of the Captain's cabin, looking fit as a fiddle now: the slight boy, not very strong; so they sent him aft, into the female latrine, to do the pouring there, while Buxton and the other bigger boy Phillips were to keep them both supplied. Bennett had a bundle of tow to use as a stopper, so that he could let the oil drip out slowly and regularly, instead of in one big wasteful splodge. You only want a very little oil to control leaping water: even for so big a ship, one drum ought to last for an hour or two.

Bennett made a dash, and managed to win the big iron slice-shaped room, with its long row of squatting-places: they rolled a drum in after him, and the big iron door clanged to. It was pitch dark, the air charged with the smell of citronella (Essential Oil had been stored there, to avoid tainting the holds). The ship's list had laid this starboard latrine down almost to water-level: and as she rolled the sea came up through the vent, gurgling like the waste of a gigantic bath, swirling about the boy's knees. He made a dash for the door, in a panic: but it would not open: the iron latch, outside, was a swing one, and the angle the ship was

103

heeled to kept it swung into the locked position: it could only be opened from without. If the ship rolled just a little more, of course, the room would fill, and drown him. Coal-miners, in an accident, have sometimes been saved from drowning by the air-pressure: fleeing to the end of an ascending gallery, the water has not been able to rise to them because there was nowhere for the present air to escape. But latrines are properly ventilated, in accordance with strict regulations: in fact are designed to drown anyone locked inside them for sure, as neat as a mouse in a mousetrap.

Well, never mind; at present it did not seem to come above his knees, and only that once in a while. So he got busy. Fixed his tow plug, broached his drum, began pouring. He could not tell if it was doing any good: only the chaps outside could tell that.

The chaps outside could see that the effect of the oil was magical. A thin film only a few molecules in thickness (once it had spread out), it bound millions of tons of water. Huge spires of water would dash at the ship, like maddened cathedrals: then the oil spread over them: they rounded, sank, passed away as harmless as a woman's bosom. Or even if they broke, it was only harmless dead water.

In an hour and a half Bennett's drum was finished: and no one came with more.

They did not come, because at the time they thought they could not. The wind was in one of its worst paroxysms. A man might manage to cross the well-deck in a wild dash emptyhanded: but not carrying a drum of oil. So the engineers started pouring it over amidships, with buckets. A wasteful way; but better than nothing, they thought.

Wasteful, and not nearly so effective. It was soon plain that somehow they *must* get a fresh lot forward to Bennett. So the Mate and Phillips accepted the risk: stood waiting their bare chance for a dash, with a drum apiece: though it still seemed impossible.

Phillips was not looking when the Mate made his dash: when he looked back, the Mate was gone.

Gone? Gone overboard, that must mean. Phillips dropped his drum and ran for the saloon. "Mate's overboard" he yelled through the door. The few engineers inside listened politely but without consternation. Then he ran back: caught up his drum and dashed for the after-castle himself: he took it to be a necessity, since he thought he was the only one left, but he hardly expected to get through.

He did, though, and wrenched open the door. Buxton tumbled out on top of him. Somehow, Phillips had been so sure that Buxton was drowned: the shock of seeing the Mate alive nearly sent the boy himself overboard.

In Hazard

Bennett had two drums now: enough to last him nearly till the evening. He settled down to the job.

It is only human to take a pride in what you are doing: to want to do it well. It is one of the chief springs of effort: pride in perfecting the means, not just the wanting the object. You expect artists and poets to have that pride: you can understand a fine craftsman—carpenter or seaman—having it. But really nearly everyone has it, whatever his job. The dustman is proud of the quality of the refuse he tends. The experienced sewerman knows that of all the careless footfalls passing above his head, not one man, not Duke nor taxi-driver, could clear a choked main drain with so deft a hand as he. You might have thought Bennett's job monotonous, dribbling oil slowly down a half-flooded latrine in the half-dark? Not a bit of it. As the hours passed his technique improved! And the improvement was itself fascinating. Just how much oil to slop in at a time. Just how far, and how often, to withdraw the tow plug, in order to let it trickle through. Just what to cling on to, when the water came up. You would have thought he would get bored? No: the fact is that the boy stuck to his post, pouring oil, without food or rest, for twenty hours on end—till mid-day Saturday: and though at the end he was so dog-tired as to be dreaming on his feet, he never felt bored.

106

Nor had it been long before dreams and technique had woven themselves together.

Most frequently he imagined himself in a lecture-room, where a dreary lecturer droned out a discourse on pouring oil. Sometimes he was himself the lecturer, explaining in balanced periods the Whole Art of Oil-pouring, its every thrust and parry and riposte; while an entranced audience of students scribbled down his sections, and subsections *a* and *b*, his riders and exceptions, in their notebooks.

A jerk of the mind, and he would find that he was in fact doing what he thought he was saying. Then a slow glissade down the slope of consciousness, till once more he believed himself to be saying what he was in fact doing.

Never, during the whole twenty hours, did it enter his head to want to give up. It is at times very difficult to draw the line between a hero and an artist. Without doubt it was the pouring of the oil which saved the ship at that time. Without doubt it was the way Bennett stuck to his post in the after latrine, and Watchett to his post in the forward one, that made the pouring of oil so successful.

When the tank of oil in the engine-room was exhausted, the engineers broke off one of those hooked ventilators I told you about, in the side decks, which release the gases from the fuel-tanks below, and thence dipped it up with buckets.

107

In Hazard

II

Perhaps it was a pity ever to have brought the engine-room Chinese up on deck at all. They had been all right below: but now they could see how bad things were. It did not do them any good. For after a while they refused even to carry the oil in the shelter of the centre-castle. They did not go comatose like the deck-hands, they went a bit ugly. This was not what they had signed on for. If this was what they were expected to go through, they ought to have been told. The English, in taking them into a storm like this without telling them when they signed on, had broken the bargain: it was as bad as lying to them. This, on top of the food ramp (they were now feeling very hungry) was more than they could be expected to stand. They gave very little sign; but one and all were ready to make serious trouble if a match was put to the powder.

Mr. MacDonald was not only sensitive about his machines: he was highly sensitive about his men. He knew at once that the loyalty of his men was gone from him, that he could not trust them. That did not do *him* any good. He took to swivelling round suddenly, with a glare of his hot red eyes, to see if there was a Chinaman behind him. Soutar, also, was on edge about it. He could see that MacDonald was nervy about the men; and he resented it. If the Chinks gave trouble, couldn't he bash them? And my God, how he would like the chance! What was the good of the Chief getting all worked up about it? Being *afraid* of them?

Two Chinamen, their faces wooden and angry, were in Soutar's way as he trundled a drum. With an unexpectedly falsetto oath he kicked out at them—and missed. They vanished. But MacDonald saw and turned on Soutar.

"Gin ye distrust the men, Mr. Soutar," he said, "can ye nae hau'd yoursel' in, an' nae shaw it?"

He, distrust them! When the Chief was in dithering terror of them!

Bitter anger burst up between the two men, who glared in each other's faces: MacDonald, half his grey moustache burnt off in the donkey-room, his eyes red-rimmed and bloodshot: Soutar, his pasty white face screwed up, and wearing a blackish hue as if diluted ink ran in his veins: his meagre eyelashes almost entirely hidden between the puffed lids.

It was at that moment Gaston spoke quietly to the Chief.

"I've got water, Sir," he said: "not much, but enough for a wet."

Water! The first for a day and a half! At the very word the glands in their gums twinged with pain.

"I thought of unscrewing the valves off the winches," Gaston explained. "There is water condensed there: a cupful or two."

(There would be, of course, from the cooling of the steam which once had turned them.)

109

In Hazard

So that was the next thing. They won the water from the winches with the scrupulous care of men winning gold from the gravel. Each man was able to wet his lips. Each man, except Watchett pouring oil in the forward latrine, and Bennett in the after one. No one remembered them.

Night was falling: the obscurity turned once more from white to black. The sea was still madly broken: oiling must without doubt continue all night.

Edwardes, with a little electric torch, examined the sheaf of notes which one day would be the ship's official log. They were scribbled on the backs of wireless forms, and stuffed into the rack for signal flags on the Bridge. Where was he? It seemed impossible to tell, except by instinct. No stars or sun for a sight, nor any hope of them. They were being carried along by the storm: but where was it taking them? Its path was anyhow so erratic, no one could tell where it might now be heading. That bank must have been Serrana or Serranilla, though . . . but where would they end up? Hurricanes are bound to hit the land sometime. When this one struck Cuba, or Yucatan, or Florida, would they still be in it?

Chapter VIII

The night which followed was one which no one would ever forget: yet one which no one could ever clearly remember.

Dick had an easier job than Bennett to keep awake: for he had not slept at all, the crust of his wakefulness was still unbroken. But in some ways he was worse off. The fo'c'sle was more battered than the poop. Bigger seas swept up through the vent. Moreover, it was a latrine that until the storm had been in use. Still, he was not imprisoned, like Bennett: the door had broken clean off.

His head ached; and his tongue, instead of being flat and moist in his mouth, was round and dry. Consequently it kept trying to push its way out between his lips, like the thin end of a wedge. Only it could not, it stuck to his lips each time, as if they were smeared with the best glue; and it had to be loosened carefully, so as not to tear the skin.

"You see," he said to Sukie, "You have to be

In Hazard

very careful. Once it gets a chance really to stick
to the skin it will rip it off. Very gently, back and
fore—that frees it, and I can put it back in my
mouth."

But Sukie did not answer: though surely she
ought to have been interested. She was looking past
him, and humming a tune. She did not care. So
with an effort of mind he shifted her out of his
way; shifted her up about four feet, and a bit to
the left. There was nothing for her to sit on up
there: but all the same there she was, sitting in
just the same position as before. Presently she did
have somewhere to sit, however, for he saw she
was now in the mouth of a ferny cave. So with a
spasm of pleasure he picked up his oil-drum and
stepped through her, into the cave, pouring oil as
he went (so as to be able to find his way back, he
told himself).

"You see," he said when he met her again, about
a hundred yards further down the cave, "pouring
oil out of this drum is my job."

"Sure," said Sukie: and leaning forward she
stared close into his eyes, laying her beautiful cool
eyes almost to touch his briny, swollen lids.

"Oh, sure!" she said again: and turning, hopped
away on her unnaturally elongated feet, nervously
folding and unfolding her ears. So he took hold
of the tow plug at the end of the cave and lifted
it; and this time quite a lot of oil ran out.

112

"I must be more careful," he thought: "I'll be using it up too soon at this rate."

But only half the drum was gone: and just then the Mate and Phillips arrived with two new drums.

"Keep one drum in reserve," said the Mate. "That's the Captain's orders."

"Very good sir," Dick tried to say, but it hurt his tongue too much. Talking to Sukie had not hurt his tongue at all.

II

The road from Fakenham Station to the town runs past a meadow, with willows.

In Dick's day an old horse-bus still traversed it, back and forth, to meet every train. The horse never did more than walk: you never saw anyone getting in, or getting out; the bus was painted black, but on the glass of the back window transparent lilies were painted.

After the willows comes a printing-works: and then the town.

In the market-place there is a chemist's shop: and the chemist is a long-established sort of chap, who knows the old-fashioned names for things. He knows that Sal Prunella is only salt-petre with the water expelled, for instance. That was useful; because Dick's mother had come across an old cookery-book, written in different hands but all at least two hundred years old, and she wanted to

113

try a recipe for curing Westphalia Hams Mrs. Estrigge. So she copied out the queer names of the things on a piece of paper and sent Dick down to the chemist for them on his bicycle.

He was only too glad of any excuse to take out his bicycle, in those days: for it was his first one, and still new. Gran'dad had said from the beginning that he might not have one till his eleventh birthday, for fear of spoiling his heart; but ever since he was five years old he had wanted one, with a burning want.

But Gran'dad was unbendable. So, going to infant-school, he would trot along, knees coming up like *haute école*, arms bent at the elbows, and his hands in front holding imaginary handle-bars, thumbing an imaginary bell at the corners. Indeed this pretended bike was so real to him that anyone who could not see it must be very dense. He never got over his contempt for the old Rector of Bensham, who had met him one day like that bicycling along in front of his mother:

"I have just seen your young man," the Rector called out genially to her as he passed, "riding by on his *horse!*"

Once he had got his real machine, Dick used to go for rides with his Gran'dad. The old man, at seventy, was still a keen biker. He used to say that he could still ride now as far as ever he could. That was probably true; for as he decayed, bikes improved. In the days of his vigorous youth he had juggled along on a Penny farthing. Then came the "safety" bicycle: but it had a fixed wheel, going down hill you still had to take your feet off the pedals if you wanted to "coast": and prudent people were chary of taking their feet off the pedals, seeing their pedals were what they chiefly relied on for braking.

Then came the free-wheel: then came the three-speed gear, in time for Gran'dad's last machine: and Dick's first bicycle, or course, had all these things.

One day, years after Gran'dad's death, Dick had found the old Penny-farthing at the back of a shed. The green paint on it was still first-class. But the bolt which held the saddle to the primitive spring was rusted, and he had a job to fix the saddle in place. And the tyres were quite perished. They were just long narrow rubber strips, like pram-tyres: they had grown too long for the wheels and fell off as soon as he moved the machine: so he bound them over and over with wire to hold them on.

When he tried to ride the thing, however, he found it almost impossibly difficult: he came hurtling off in the second yard. Good lord! Was this the thing Gran'dad used to ride all over the country as a matter of course? As he rubbed his shins he reflected, for the first time, that after all Gran'dad was not born old: must once have been even nimble, like himself.

In Hazard

He had seen photos of him, in black whiskers and tight knickerbockers, perched easily on this very machine. But he had always taken for granted that the machine must be easy to ride, if Gran'dad could do it (like the tricycle which old Archdeacon Bubble used to trundle to Church every Sunday, at a walking pace). So it was very upsetting to find this machine, which Grandfather had once ridden with such sangfroid, pitching him head over heels again and again: and he determined to master it.

That meant long, secret practice: and in the end of course he succeeded.

There came the day of a cricket-match, when everyone was very excited, and inclined to think up impromptu Comic Acts. So Dick slipped home, and dressed in some very old-fashioned clothes of his dead grandfather's. Then he got out the Penny-farthing, and presently did a very comic Act indeed on it, riding round the Marketplace in an exaggerated manner while both teams cheered and jeered. He felt a pretty bright chap to be able to make them laugh like that: but he felt a bit less bright when presently he saw his Mother standing there; watching him make a fool of her old dead father, who had always been very fond of him. It was not a comfortable moment.

It was almost as bad as that other time, when he thought she had heard him boasting about what he did at Holy Communion. He was telling

116

some other boys he had drunk up all the wine
that Sunday, with the Rector pulling at the Cup
but him hanging on. It was untrue: in point of
fact, he always behaved in Church with strict de-
cency, and indeed was very devout and believing
—especially about the Holy Spirit being present
at Communion. Yet he had boasted it, in a wild
fit, to outshine the bad boys who were listening
—and then, turning, saw his Mother standing just
behind him. What was he to do? She might never
have heard at all; so he could not just take her
aside and assure her it was not true. He had to
wait for her to make the first move. But she made
no move, she never mentioned it. Did that mean
she had not heard? Or was she too deeply shocked
to be able to speak of it? The uncertainty made
him avoid her; and for the first time he took to
locking the bathroom door against her while he had
a bath.

Most boys are inclined to be decently devout
the year of their Confirmation: Dick was perhaps
actually more devout than the average. It sprang
from the experiences of his childhood. For he had
found, when very young, that if he prayed for something he wanted badly, he nearly always got it.
Or, if he was not to have it, he was never left in
doubt: God let him know at once, even while he
was praying—but as a rule God gave him whatever he asked. And he, for his part, moved by a
decent compunction, never made too unreasonable

requests (he never asked for a premature bicycle, for instance, for God and Gran'dad had too much in common). Again, he found God a most ready companion, always at hand when called on in dark passages and up dark stairs.

I do not mean that this child lived always in close communion with his God; never felt doubts, times when God was faint to him. Children only feel *implicit* belief in something they have called out of their own imaginations, such as an imaginary playfellow, or a lion in the shrubbery. Any existence, such as God's, which comes to their experience from outside, is bound to be more shadowy than that. He had his Mother's word for it, that there is a God: and her word was backed by the evidence of all his answered prayers, of that felt company in the dark. But evidence is not the same as direct experience: God could never be so certain a fact as his imagined bike. He could never visualise God; beyond a fleeting vision of black whiskers and tight knickerbockers.

But in time these beliefs, these doubts, came to a climax. It was over the business of his watch.

He was ten years old then, and going to a boys' day-school. He walked there alone. Part of his way lay down a private road; the end of which, to prevent through-traffic, was barred by a scaffold-pole lashed to trestles. He was in the habit of doing gymnastics on this bar for a few minutes, as he passed, going and coming. While he turned his somersaults, he used to lay his watch carefully on the ground.

One night, when he went to bed, he found his watch was not in his pocket. In a flash he remembered that he had never picked it up again after his spell of gymnastics on the way home that day. That was hours ago. Any number of people passed down that road: it was inconceivable that the watch had not already been found and pinched. And yet . . . might it be worth trying? He got out of his bed, and knelt down beside it.

Before mentioning the watch, he told God frankly that there had been many times, lately, when he had doubted the whole fact of God's existence. He wanted to get the matter settled. Let this be a test case. I have told you that a compunction had always prevented him from asking anything too difficult, anything with a touch of the miraculous in it. So all those answered prayers might be only coincidence. But this prayer would be different: there was plenty of the miraculous in this one, since it would have to act backwards. He was asking God to guard his watch during all those hours which were already past! As a test case it was perfect: and he for his part was ready to make a promise. If God would, against all likelihood, guard his watch, hide it both from the eyes which had passed and the eyes which would pass, so that he found it still lying in the same place in the road on his way to school in the morning—

why, he would then give an irrevocable promise never, so long as he lived, to doubt God's existence again. That is what he prayed.

In the morning he found the watch, lying just where he had put it, in the road. So thenceforth he was pledged, for the rest of his life, to believe in God.

It is curious that having done one miraculous thing by prayer, he did not go on to others. But his compunction still held him. That had been a special occasion, necessary to settle his faith. No further miracles—however convinced he was that by prayer he could do them—might be justified. I pass over such temptations as one which came to him, on a day when the whole school were cooped in by a wet afternoon, to fly slowly across the classroom. That was obviously reprehensible: and so, easily resisted. But there came another that was not so easy.

Coming out of the post-office one day ahead of his Mother, he found himself close up against a sort of flat trolley, as flat as a table, on which a little girl lay under bed-clothes as if in bed. He had seen her before, at a distance, wheeled through the streets like this: and his Mother had told him she had a disease of the spine, and would never again walk, or even sit up: but he had never before been confronted with her close. Her face was pale, and moist; and rather proud.

120

Suddenly his whole being was possessed by a single thought. He had only to stretch out his hand and touch her, and she would rise up whole. He lifted his hand, in act to stretch it out upon her. And then, compunction spoke. He could do it: but he had no right to do it. And something other than compunction spoke. If he did this, what would be the sequel? A little boy who has once done a miracle in a crowded street cannot turn back, and live again the life of other boys. No more sweets and chucking ink-bombs. He would be someone apart, from then on: pledged to the utmost holiness of living, given over to saving mankind from its sins. It is not only the Devil who buys souls: if God did this for him, his soul would be sold to God for that price, every instant of his future dedicated to burn in the intensity of God's service.

Could he drink of that cup?

He lowered his hand, and passed on with leaden heart; for he knew he was leaving the little girl to more years of pain, and presently to death. That he might be doing right: but that he was being a kind of murderer.

Suppose she knew that he had this power: knew that he was deliberately refusing to save her!

—But by now his Mother had joined him. Her next call was the newspaper shop, where she bought him half an ounce of that kind of liquorice all-sorts he most loved.

In Hazard

III

The promise he had given seemed simple enough to keep, to a child of ten. But the trouble was that Dick did not remain always a child of ten: he grew. It seems that as you grow, God must grow too. Of this of course he was not forewarned: that the God he had promised to believe in for ever was a child's God.

When he was fifteen, and being prepared for Confirmation, the idea of God which was presented to him for belief was very different: a sort of impersonal Omnipotence Who never interfered with Science (not that He could not, but simply because He was above that sort of thing, and meant us to learn Boyle's Law and so on): a vague, limitless Holiness, Who really preferred the Church of England to anything else but Who failing that was also the Best Elements in all religions (especially Buddhism and Islam). In short, not at all the sort of God you asked for small material benefits, like looking after your watch for you, or helping you to win a football match. In fact, surely a different sort of God altogether. And—here was the difficulty—*not* the God he was pledged to believe in, because not the God which the evidence, still vividly remembered, had once so clearly affirmed.

What was he to do? Everyone assumed that he could no longer, at his age, believe in the God of his childhood. Such faith was all very well for a child, but not for an intelligent, educated lad. In fact, if he tried to carry such a belief through life all the most religious people—beginning with the good old man whose classes he was attending—would seriously disapprove. They would call it the crudest sort of bigotry, if not downright wicked, if he continued to believe that God was on his side. God, *they* said, was on nobody's side.

Well, he supposed they knew: and he conscientiously tried to believe as they taught him, against his instinct. In this new God. It seemed, the only proper thing to pray for, to this God, was Grace: i.e. to be made gooder. So he only prayed for Grace. But he could see little result. And in this he was not greatly surprised: for the one prayer of his childhood which had never been answered was the formal prayer he prayed every night, "Make me a good boy." He had never found that his behaviour next day was a whit the better for it.

IV

It was dark. Dick had been pouring oil for ten hours now, and he was sick of it. He did it automatically, so it could not hold his thoughts. And his thoughts now turned to the thin steel plates which were all that lay between him and the fury of the waters. Once more, he was afraid. How crassly confident people were, to build ships and take it for granted they would float, even on top of miles and miles of water! It was all a question of weights, of course. They said the ship's weight exactly balanced the weight of water it displaced. But to his mind, now grown so giddy, mere balance suddenly ceased to seem very re-assuring. A thing which was balanced could be upset. That Penny-farthing balanced, if you knew how: yet he had upset off it often enough. Suppose now the ship's balance was upset? I mean, suppose she grew heavier, or the water grew lighter? Down she would go like a stone. What fools folk are, to go on building great ships, and sending them out onto the sea; taking for granted that they will all float because one has: taking for granted that because a ship floats one day she will float the next: never thinking how easily that balance of weights might be upset.

Indeed, there seemed to his mooning mind little reason why the "Archimedes" should not give up floating any minute of any voyage—even if there were not the storm to consider.

Storm? His mind reeled and turned over, waking a few degrees. Of course, it was the *storm* which was the danger—that about balance was rubbish. But the storm was not rubbish. He suddenly realised that the latrine he was in was changing shape. The walls were closer in. As iron bends under the blows of the hammer, so this iron was flattening, under the blows of the sea. It was beginning to bulge inwards.

124

Friday

Dick had not prayed for material things for many years, because he had thought it was wrong. In his heart of hearts he still believed he would get them, if he did: but when you are grown up you have no business praying for them. So God, while granting your prayer, would probably see it went bad on you: would give you ample cause to wish you had never asked for the thing. Grace was all you were supposed to ask for, and general spiritual well-being. But oh, Sweet Lord! It was not spiritual well-being he wanted just now, he wanted to bloody well not be drowned in his twenty-first year.

He got down on his knees, with his arm braced round a pillar, and prayed till he sweated, there in the forward starboard latrine:

"Oh Lord God, I was a fool ever to go to sea. Oh Lord God, get me back home safe off it. Oh Lord God, I do most heartily repent of my wasted years, and of what I thought about when I was shut in my room instead of Thee—Oh Lord God don't hold that against me, don't drown me because of that. Oh Lord God, I pray Thee, save me off the sea!"

But then misgivings assailed him. Suppose God did save him: gave him the bare thing he asked, but turned it bad on him? Saved him from drowning only to perish at once in a house-on-fire, or be hanged? How had he better put it? Glimmerings

of his Confirmation-teaching began to come back
to him:

"Oh Lord," he went on, "that is to say, only
save me from drowning if that be already Thy
Will: at any rate, don't let it be to my harm to be
saved from drowning: and if Thou savest me, use
the rest of my life for Thy purposes, not as it has
been up to now."

That apparently was all right: for at that moment he felt a most distinct and stabbing promise,
of the kind he remembered so well, that he should
be saved alive kindly.

To make his praying more intense, he ground
his knuckles hard into his eyes. The pain was almost unbearable: his eyes being cracked and inflamed, and his hands smeared with engine-oil
and salt.

Then he got back to work again.

V

Then he got back to work again, and after a while
the heroic part he was filling dawned upon him,
as he poured the saving oil, in single-handed com-
bat for his ship against the whole wrath of the sea.
It was light again now, it must be morning: a grey
light filled the latrine. He had been at his post
since early yesterday afternoon, without relief: it
would soon be twenty-four hours. And indeed he
had been on duty with the rest of them, without

126

sleep or rest, for four whole days and nights (or was it only three?).

If only Sukie could see him now! No shore-going uniform and brass buttons, like a tailor's dummy; but stripped and steely, fighting the storm with a superhuman strength, a dour devotion to duty. Hour after hour, hour after hour. Day after day. Indefatigable. Surely, if she could see him like this, she would love him with her whole heart?

And yet, I don't know. Would she have loved him? She had liked well enough to sit on the knees of his shore-going uniform, to rub her cheek against his pink smooth cheek. Would she really have preferred to sit on the knees of oily and sodden dungarees, her cheek against his sore and stubbly jaw?

His face did not wear, as he thought, the lean, drawn, and lion-like aspect one expects of an unflinching hero. For the immediate effect on a hero's face of unflinching effort is seldom to make him look romantic. More often it makes him look liverish. You know that noble look of open, wise patience, that you have seen on the face of some great explorer? That look did not come to him in the desert. The desert may have begotten it, but it only came to him afterwards, in safety and comfort. In the desert he looked at times brutal, at times petulant, at times frightened. Never noble.

If Sukie heard of all this afterwards, told graphically, so that she could imagine the scene according to her own ideas, then indeed it might sway her towards him. But not if she had been there.

For lift Dick for a moment out of his surroundings, and give him the once-over. It is hard to tell the immediate effects of heroism from those of indulgence. With nothing but appearances to go on, you would probably guess that figure to be one of Life's Failures, who, sodden with drink, had spent the night on a garbage pile. His face now was dirty, swollen, puffy, weak-looking—in fact, ugly and pretty contemptible. And he smelt disgusting.

Chapter IX

"Archimedes" carried plenty of engineers, more engineers than deck-officers: and now there was very little for them to do. During the early part of the storm they had congregated in the saloon: but as the conflict deepened they withdrew from there, one by one, and congregated on the engine-flat. The deck-officers could not understand that: could not understand why, when the ship was in peril, they should like to penetrate down there where they had no hope of escape; where they would not even know she was sinking, if she did, until she did. The engineers for their part could not understand why the deck-officers should prefer to remain high up, near the open deck, where you were almost exposed to the storm itself.

I suppose really both had the same reason for what they did. Each wanted to be in a familiar place. For surely you feel safest in your most familiar place. A small child, in the dark, feels wholly safe in his own bed: would rather face the lion in the room from his bed (from which there is no chance of escape) than standing barefoot near the door with a chance of bolting down the passage if it springs.

So the engineers, with common accord, took their station by their sleeping engines; and indeed Mr. MacDonald had never left that station.

Mr. MacDonald had a mattress brought down for him: but I do not say that he passed an easy night. He could not close his eyes. I do not mean just that he could not sleep: he could not close his eyes. They felt as if the lids were propped apart with short lengths of stick. He tried closing them with his fingers, but they would not stay shut: released, the lids crept back off the ball.

Most of the night his mind tried to run on water, the water he would drink if he could: but instead, fiery were the things he saw. The dead furnaces were shooting out flames again (as they did when they were blowing back): and every flame a Chinaman. Chinamen were licking round his knees, trying to catch them. Blasts of Chinamen burst from each furnace-door: or ran in coveys squealing across the floors, like rats in a hold. Some of them took lengths of cotton waste to tie round the steering-rods, and jam into the joints, for fear these steering-rods might ever again be used: others, flying by in threes with a buzz, alighted on the turbines and the reducing-gear, and drawing the corkscrews that were hidden in their trousers used them to prise out the most vital parts, which, turned soft and succulent in their hands, they ate irrevocably,

Do not think Mr. MacDonald was asleep. I told you the poor chap could not even shut his eyes. He saw these things with his eyes open, long after he had left his mattress and was parading round and round the place. He told Soutar about them: but Soutar was too angry to care whether his Chief was mad or sane. But he too had his suspicions: and all night they kept up an endless round, for fear of what the filthy Chinese might do in anger and treacherousness to the engines.

Gaston was asleep, dog-asleep, when MacDonald woke him by shaking.

"Fetch me a cup of water," ordered the Chief: but when Gaston fell asleep again without answering he let him bide. For he could see a cascade of good water bursting out of the engine-room telegraph. Only, when he got near, he found a China-man had drunk the lot.

Mr. MacDonald had a little villa outside Ciren-cester, where he lived when on leave: a wife with a rather red face, and with grey hair strained straight up from her forehead over a brownish, sausage-shaped pad. Yet they had three children of only school-age, for they had married rather late. As the cloud of Chinamen cleared and his mind grew more lucid, it was of this he thought: and especially of his pride, the three children, hopping home from school in good outer clothes, and good

131

warm underclothes, well-fed and confident that the world was their oyster, their faces shining with unintelligence and unawakened sex. How deeply he resented their security, while he, their father, was waiting to go down in the sea! For they would never understand that the price of each little suit of winter-weight all-wool underwear was an hour of this hell. They thought it was just money: but it was not, it was his life, and they were sucking it out of his old bones, but he could no more stir and escape than the soil can escape from around the guzzling roots of a tree.

"I'm worth ten of those kids," he suddenly remarked out loud, with feeling.

Of course he was: there was so much more of him. For in the long run, if you want to say how much of a chap there is you can only measure his memory. The more he has in his memory the more of a chap there is. By that reckoning the old are often huge, and the young, for all their vanity, midgets. For surely somebody's person—well, it is the whole content of his mind. And there is very little in anybody's mind, at any time, except memory: the mind is nine parts memory, just as a jelly-fish is nine parts water.

And yet it is supposed to be a terribly sad thing, when a young man dies: but quite right and proper when an old one does! The old man dying gets little sympathy, he ought not to mind it. But does he mind it!

I expect you have seen people die: a young man bite his lip, and go out—pouf! like falling off a horse. Why, the giddy things will often go out of their way to take risks with death. But MacDonald had also once seen an old woman, aged eighty-six, on her death-bed. *She* fought for her life as a mother-tigress fights. Her last words were, as her last sun set: "I do hope I wake up alive in the morning!" Though Heaven knows what she thought she was going to wake up to. Her legs had already been dead for three days.

After all, which would you rather lose: an empty purse, or one you had spent laborious years in filling? Look what she was losing: memories of more than eighty years. But when a child dies, people get quite lyrical in their pity. Yet it is a very small loss to the child, his life: a small shimmering bagatelle. A purse with only twopence in it, and an I.O.U.

All the old know this, in an inarticulate way: Mr. MacDonald knew it: and revolved it, in deep indignation, as he paced the engine-room. But then a sudden new thought struck him. Was death in fact the end?

All his life he had been a religious man: had believed in God: had believed in Sin. But did he believe in a future life? He had really hardly considered it. He believed in Heaven and Hell, of course. But was that a real future life, or was it just a manner of speaking, a sort of Sanctions?

In Hazard

Yes, this was a new idea altogether. When his body went down in the deep, would his soul come out of it like a bubble, and rise to the top? Not only an impersonal soul, a wisp of spiritual vapour, but the actual essential him, the only William Ramsay MacDonald? Michty me! If there was any real hope of that, things were not quite so dark as they looked, not by a long chalk! He began, for the first time in his life, to wonder just what sort of a place Heaven really was.

"Mr. Soutar," he said, when the two sentries met on their beat, "dae ye beleeve in a future life?"

Mr. Soutar paused and considered carefully before answering.

"Aye," he said brusquely, and went on with his beat.

But the next time they met, it was Soutar who stopped MacDonald.

"It's nae sae easy," he said, "the subjeck is crammt wi' deeficoolties. Ye mean a future life o' a pairsonal kin', A tak' it? Me, William Edgar Soutar, and you, William Ramsay MacDonald?"

"Cairtainly," said Mr. MacDonald.

"A future life for every man born o' wumman?"

"For every Chreestian," Mr. MacDonald amended.

"Weel, noo. Are we to tak' it that a human Chreestian is compoondit o' three pairts; his body, his min', an' his speerit?"

MacDonald grunted.

134

"The body dees, the speerit leeves?"

MacDonald grunted again.

"Than whit o' the min'? That's nayther speerit nor body. Yet it's vera boont up wi' the body. A disease o' the body can disease the min'. A blow on the body can blot oot the min'. The min', like the body, graws auld an' decays. The daith o' the body, than: is that the daith o' the min' tae?"

"Allooin' it be," said MacDonald.

"Than the future life canna be of a vera pairsonal nature, A'm thinkin': it is a saft, imbecile sort o' thing ma speerit would be wi'oot ma min': nae William Edgar Soutar at a'."

He turned again on his beat: for an hour they talked no more when they met. Then MacDonald stopped him with a hand on his shoulder:

"Mr. Soutar," he said, "the human min' is hingt on reason: whit is ayont reason, reason canna camprehen'. Mebbe in the Next Worrl' we shall cast reason, as a growing bairn casts his nappies."

Soutar tore himself free and passed on. It was not till they met again he could allow himself to speak: and when he did his words burst out in passion:

"The Almichty gied us Reason tae be the only pairt in Diveenity we hae, not to be despisit! Man, ye're taukin' lik' a Sotheran!"

Once more the two men glared in each other's faces with apoplectic hate; and then passed by each other on their endless round.

135

In Hazard

II

As soon as it was light, Captain Edwardes saw with relief that they were in deep water again. The colour of the water showed it, and the more natural shape of the seas. Nevertheless he deemed it prudent to go on oiling. For he estimated that now no less than a thousand tons of water had gone below through the broken hatches: and totting up this and that, it seemed likely that all she could be expected to hold in her belly was some twelve hundred tons. The margin was getting very small.

Moreover, this deep water might not last long. Serrana Bank and Serranilla are only the southeasterly outposts (with Quito Sueno and Baxo Nuevo) of a long line of banks and cays, that stretch from Cape Gracias a Dios, in Central America, right across to the shores of Jamaica: Halfmoon Reef and Gorda Bank, Thunder Knoll and Rosalind Bank, and the great Pedro Bank with Portland Rock. If this was Serranilla he had passed, Rosalind Bank must be under his lee. And even when all the banks were passed, whither was he drifting? The Yucatan Channel is only a little more than a hundred miles wide, from Cape Catoche to Cape San Antonio. What hope was there of striking it, and so winning the open waters of the Gulf of Mexico, without being blown on the shores of either Yucatan or Cuba?

However, that was looking too far ahead. Roughly, where was he now? He must be two hundred and fifty miles or so to the eastward of Cape Gracias: driving into more shoal water: and the storm was not abating. This was the fourth day they had been in it.

Just as the engineers had been drawn to the engine-room, so now Captain Edwardes and Mr. Buxton met on the Bridge.

Mr. Buxton checked Captain Edwardes's figures in his head: that she had taken a thousand tons of water, and twelve hundred was all she could take: and agreed. He further reflected a rather curious fact. Her list was somewhat less than it had been. That was because the weight of water in the bottom of the holds now tended to balance the weight of the saturated cargo above. But suppose their pumps had been working from the first? It was the free water at the bottom of the ship that would have been first pumped out. And with nothing to counteract the weight above, she might easily have turned right over. What a mistake that would have been, to use the pumps too freely! But what an easy mistake to make.

Captain Edwardes, his fingers thrust between his belt and his belly, was even managing to pace the Bridge after a fashion. His grey chin was stubbled, his cheeks drooped: but his eye was bright and birdlike. Buxton noticed the Captain's trousers: almost the only ones of the whole ship's company not cut off at the knee: and remembering how it was his own example had stampeded that foolish trimming, blushed again to himself.

Wherein lay the man's confidence? That was what puzzled Buxton.

Few men's powers remain equable, in the face of danger. It was one of the rare qualities of Mr. Buxton himself that his did so. An efficient officer in danger, as he was an efficient officer in safety: so disciplined to his calling that neither could tamper with his abilities. But Captain Edwardes was not quite like that.

Most men are weakened by danger: when acting under its stress they are like runners carrying weight: they tire more easily. But there are a few who are strengthened by it; whose minds and bodies can only work at their highest pitch under its stimulus. Most men, if suddenly facing a loaded gun with the knowledge that they must instantly tell a lie, lie far more feebly and haltingly than they lie in a smoking-room. But a few will lie instantly and brilliantly, with an invention they normally do not possess. That was the Captain's kind. He was a good captain, at most times: but under the stimulus of danger he was rather more.

Buxton had always liked Captain Edwardes; but he had no idea before what a giant the man was inside.

It seemed that the warmth of the Mate's feeling was sensible: for at that moment, facing him, the Captain halted: dragged his right hand free from its task of supporting his fatigued abdomen, that sagged uncomfortably against the front of his trousers: grasped Buxton's hand, and shook it.

"Tell them to keep up the oiling for a while yet," he said: and watched Mr. Buxton go. That was a chief officer of sterling quality: cool, calm, fearless . . . (for in his head Edwardes was already rehearsing his Report to the Owners).

Another calculating thought struck Buxton, as he made his way aft. Suppose the funnel had not gone, when it did? Suppose those guys had held, to more than their theoretic strength? A sailing ship has been laid on her beam-ends with nothing aloft but her bare poles, before now. The resistance of that enormous funnel would have been even greater, in proportion. If the funnel had not gone, and eased her, might not the ship have turned over?

He had already seen, with horror, how each attempt they made to save themselves only invented a new danger. Now it appeared, on the other hand, that up till now it was their worst disasters which had saved them.

III

Happy, happy, happy. Duwch, Captain Edwardes was happy as a sand-boy! Had he known, at the beginning, what was coming, would he have been happy and confident like this all through? Perhaps not. Perhaps no one could have borne that foreknowledge. But passing instead from each known moment only to the unknown moment ahead, his happiness had carried him along.

He had a million or so pounds' worth of ship and cargo to handle: and eighty men's lives. And very little chance, but that he would lose them. It was the hugeness of the responsibility which made his heart so light.

IV

At noon they were in the heart of the centre again. But there were no birds this time.

The sky too was different. Instead of a stormy black, it was an even and luminous grey, a shining grey. But the heat and the thinness of the air were as melancholy as ever. You could have sat down and wept, if your eyes had not been too dry.

There was no living thing to see. No birds. No sharks. The oil-bound water heaved like Styx. Buxton, looking down into that rolling murk with its thin rainbow skin, would have welcomed even the grin of a shark as evidence that the world had not ended.

They were all gathered on the deck, even the oilers at last taking a spell. They did what they could for the hatches, in a dreamy way: but you had little will in that air, and they were short of timber now.

It was a strange thing, that when so much had smashed away over the side several of the life-boats

140

were still there. Life-boats carry emergency rations, biscuit and water: or they should. So Captain Edwardes now set some of them to searching: and they found what they were looking for: barrels of biscuit, and water-jars.

Water was what they wanted first. But water-jars are stopped with wooden stoppers, which are inclined to shrink and work loose. Then in a big buffeting they work out. This had happened. They found plenty of water-jars, but very little water; and what there was, tainted with brine; some useless to drink, only a very little that was good. They shared it out, and then turned to the biscuit.

Most of the barrels had leaked, or burst. Still, they did get some biscuit.

Mr. MacDonald, singed and glaring, reeled about the deck, a useless biscuit in each hand. Useless? "It is a' vera weel for youse young anes," he croaked wildly: "but ha'e ye ever tried to eat ship's biscuit wi' fa'se teeth?"—And the emptiness in his belly seemed to be knocking with the rhythmic blows of a hammer.

Down below, in the refrigerator, there were lashings of food. Meat, eggs, butter, salads, everything you could want. All down there in the fridge. "Shall I *try* to open the fridge, Sir?" the Chief Steward asked the Captain. But Captain Edwardes said no. Once open, everything inside would be spoilt. As long as there was flood-water round the door, the fridge must not be opened.

141

In Hazard

Although, of course, with the electricity cut off it would not be long before everything inside spoilt anyhow.

So for the eleventh time the Chief Steward routed round his pantry, searching in every nook and cranny: and this time he found something. He found an apple and an orange, and he took them to the captain.

Captain Edwardes started to eat half the orange, meaning to keep the other half for the Mate. But once he tasted it his jaws took charge. He could not stop, he ate it all. When he knew what he had done, he sought out the Mate.

He found him, and gave him the apple, and said to him, "Mr. Buxton, I've played you a dirty trick. There was an orange too, and I ate it all."

Chapter X

Mr. Buxton, sucking his apple on the bridge, suddenly realised for the first time why he had gone to sea (he had been at sea now for twenty-five years). It was because he liked virtue: and was not the Economic Man.

The Economic Man sells his labour, at a rate of money. Work is something he is prepared to do, in fair proportion to the money he gets for it. His working day is the number of hours he is willing to waste, in order to have the wherewithal to live and to enjoy his leisure.

The man with a profession also calls what he does "work": but his meaning is exactly opposite. It is the hours he is not working which he considers wasted. Pay? Of course he expects to be paid: a man cannot live on air. But whereas the Economic Man looks on work as the means to get money, the professional man looks on money as the means to do work.

—All this is too simple: but it is the gist of the

conclusions Mr. Buxton now came to. The gist only, for being so hungry he thought in jerks, flashes of insight which were not connected up as I am putting them here.

That was one reason why he had gone to sea. Sea-going is almost the only profession open to the poor man.

As a profession, though, sea-going seems something of an anomaly: for is not its mainspring Trade? Yes, it is a Colossus with each foot planted in a different set of values. I mean, the *raison d'être* of it is economic, and yet the practice of it is judged by standards which are not economic at all, which can only be called moral: and which are peculiar to it. For the working of a ship calls for certain qualities—virtues, if you like—which do not seem to be appropriate to-day to the relations of employers and employed on shore. The shore-labourer's liability is limited: the seaman's is unlimited. The seaman may be called on to give the utmost that he is able, even to laying down his life. That is not an imposition on him, a piece of chicanery on the part of his employers: it is inherent in the profession he practises. A necessary draw-back?— Oddly enough, it even seems to be the reason why certain men, such as Mr. Buxton, embrace that profession in the first place.

I can only suppose that Virtue (using the word in its Roman rather than its Victorian sense) is a natural instinct with some men: they really cannot be happy unless they can give it an outlet.

Moreover, this professional attitude is not confined to the seaman himself; it is an infection which spreads right through the business of shipping, and crops up in the most unlikely places: even in board-rooms. For you would think the Owners at least would be Economic Men, bent solely on their own enrichment? Enrich-me-quicks are common among them, of course. Yet some Owners are not enrich-me-quicks. They all draw very substantial salaries out of the business, it is true, and live in a handsome and solid way: but often it is not a tenth of what they could squeeze out, if they really regarded the Fleet as their sponge. They draw out what they need, to keep up the state of Lord Mayor or whatever has fallen to them: all the rest they put back into their ships. It appears they would rather have fine ships than fine wives, fine pleasures —fine anything else.

This common professional attitude to sea-going both sides of the pay-desk has one odd result. The seamen come to expect almost as high a standard of conduct from the Owners as from each other. Every act of the Owners will be assessed by the whole fleet, and rigorously judged. Nor will the verdict be hidden, for expediency. If an Owner's virtue (again, the Roman sense) is found lacking, his officers may be so ashamed as to want to hide their heads: but they will not pretend they have not noticed the fault.

—But this is wandering a little from the course of Buxton's meditations, as he stood holding to the bridge-rail, the wind and the incessant noise battering him from without, hunger and weariness battering him from within, yet a comfortable sort of contentment suffusing the thin, hollow shell between the two.

II

The wind roared, and the gigantic feathered sea curled down out of the sky: but in the shelter of the fo'c'sle a small young cold Chinaman clung to the remnant of a derrick. Suds swirled almost up to his waist, at times: but his pocked face was earnest, busy and detached. He was trying to light fireworks.

They were addressed to the Heavenly Consort, the Lady T'ien Fei. For she alone of the celestial company (except perhaps Kuan-yin herself) has power to control that old, panting, huge yellow-and-white bag, the Dragon of the Winds.

T'ien Fei was once a little girl, precocious and devout, and subject to fits. She was born in the island of Mei-chow, in Fukien, in A.D. 742. At five years old she could recite the prayers of Kuan-yin-pu-sa, and at eleven could perform the dance called Ngan-chieh-lo-shen. In one of her trances, her spirit went to the aid of her four brothers, who were caught by

146

a storm in small boats, far from home. They actually saw their sister walking towards them on the water: but then she vanished. For at that moment her parents, growing anxious, had recalled her spirit to her body, with gongs. They had recalled her too soon, she told them: her brothers were in danger, and only three of them had she had time to save (the fourth, in very fact, never came home).

She was still a child when she died.

But her mission was not finished. No gongs, now, could recall her spirit when it walked on the face of the sea. Again and again, when a storm raged and the poor sailors' hearts grew weak, they would see her walking towards them on the water, and calming the water as she walked. Unofficially, she became the patron saint of sailors, and chapels to her sprang up on many dangerous coasts. Early in the twelfth century she saved the life of an Imperial ambassador: and so her sanctity, long popular, became at last official: the Emperor, being pope of their religion, canonised her (thereafter, any Chinese Grace Darling was liable to become identified with T'ien Fei).

Now, in the year 1929, young P'ing Tiao, himself born on the green shores of her native Fukien, struggled with damp gunpowder to call her aid.

His friend, Ao Ling, who had no such beliefs, watched him from the door of the centre-castle with bitter contempt.

In Hazard

It was altogether too much for Ao Ling. In a fit of uncommon rage he sprang out onto the well-deck, dashed the fizzling rubbish from P'ing Tiao's hand, drove him with blows back before him to the centre-castle.

There was something of a babel going on in there, by lantern-light. The deck-hands were sitting up on their hams: for after the noon lull they had not altogether collapsed again. The engine-room staff were standing over them, doing most of the talking. The pebbly ripple, the cheerful groaning, and the twanging, of Chinese talk.

Ao Ling listened to it, his straight black hair sticking forward over his small broad face, without putting his oar in.

The chief haranguer was Henry Tung, a Christian. He looked as if he was making an ardent speech: but in fact he was being funny about his emptiness. There was plenty of wind outside, he said: but he had more inside. He was hungry enough to swallow the whole ship. But if he did, she would not just get her funnel blown out. There was enough wind inside him to blow her plate from plate.

"Ah, wind!" said young P'ing Tiao: "Can't you talk of anything but wind?"

For answer, the Christian brought out a great artificial belch, that seemed to roll on for ever. Then, with a swift change of mood:

"Oh you young lads!" he went on, "what do

148

you know about wind? You think this a big storm?
I tell you I've been through worse than this in a
little junk! Run before it, with all sail set. Presently we saw a cow, swimming in the sea. Just then
a real bad gust blew: and while I was watching,
believe me or not, it blew the horns right out of
that cow's head! So I called to my nephew Ah-
Fêng, who was my mate: 'Ah-Fêng,' I said, 'did
you see that cow? Shall we shorten sail too?' 'You
know best, Elder Uncle,' said Ah-Fêng. 'Then hold
on!' I said. 'I don't shorten sail for any wind that
blows!'—So we held on. Then suddenly Ah-Fêng
shouts out he could see an island, right ahead.
'Helm hard up!' he shouts. 'Hard up it is!' I answered: '—Come aft, you turtle, and let her bows
rise!' So he ran aft, and sure enough her bows rose:
for he is fat as a tax-collector. That gave the wind
a chance to lift her. Up she went, cleared the island
like a swallow. Not a tree so much as brushed her
keel. 'Now go forward,' I said, as soon as we were
over: 'we don't want to go to Heaven yet!' So Ah-
Fêng walks forward, gentle and cautious; and down
she comes on the water without even a splash.''

Mr. Soutar, hidden in the gloom, listened and
watched.

No one who has been (as Mr. Soutar had)
through a Chinese mutiny, wishes to do so again.
Such mutinies take a little time to work up: but
when they do burst, the change which comes over
the men is extraordinary—and horrible. It is a

149

crowd-effect; impersonal, like the change in water when it boils. Kind, happy-go-lucky, decent chaps, with a sense of humour, go insanely cruel: with the faces of devils. And their horrible screaming all the time. If they have knives in their hands they simply cannot refrain from cutting at you, even while you are talking to them. They will cut at any little unimportant bit of you they can get at, if your vital parts are out of reach.

The *only* thing is to try and arrest the trouble in time.

Mr. Soutar could not understand a word of Chinese: but he believed that you can sometimes divine more surely what men are talking about if you do not understand a single word, than if you have a small smattering of their tongue. You rely on your eyes alone, to note the expression of their faces: and the tones of their voices help you.

He had never trusted that fat Hong-Kong Christian greaser, Henry Tung. He disliked all Mission-boys on principle: it never does to trust them. Now look at that chap: it was plain as a pike-staff what he was up to. A born demagogue and agitator. No need to be a sinologue to tell he was working the men up to some devilment: machine-wrecking, mutiny, murder—you could *see* the sort of thing he was urging!

—For Henry, his face very solemn indeed, his eyes pleading for belief, was telling one whopper

150

after another: and the group of men listened to him fascinated, eyes wide and shining.

"Did I ever tell you," said Henry, "how I once had a drinking-match with a tiger?"

"My God!" thought Soutar: "If I was captain I'd shoot that man where he stands: nip the whole thing in the bud!"

"My God!" thought Soutar, "If only I knew Chinese I should have him! But if I tackle him now, he'll only deny he was preaching mutiny at all!"

Then, quietly as he had come, Mr. Soutar crept away again, to look for the Captain.

III

The powerful innate forces in us, the few prime movers common to us all, are essentially plastic and chameleonlike. The shape and colour which they come to present at the mind's surface bear little seeming relation to the root: appear characteristic rather of the medium through which they have struggled to the light.

Where men's environment, their education, differ fundamentally, flowers from the same hidden root will *seem* to bear no kinship: will differ "fundamentally" too.

Take that curious opposition, and tension (or at least tie), which exist in all men, and indeed in all beasts, between parent and child. The form in

151

which it emerges into behaviour is (speaking broadly) a matter of cultural environment. Amongst Anglo-Saxons, it flowers today for the most part in revolt: in an exaggerated contempt of the adolescent child for the parent: a contempt far greater than he would feel for any other human being of the same calibre as his father. Amongst the Chinese, it is precisely this same root which flowers in obedience, in worship of the parent. In both cases the root is the same: a tie felt to be immensely strong, and potentially very painful: so, *we* tug against that tie, desperately, trying to snap it, while *they* walk towards the source of the pull faster than the pull itself, so leaving the cord quite slack!

The Englishman, because he does not have to obey his parents (once he is an adult), often hates them: while the Chinaman, because he has to obey them implicitly, seldom hates them.

Sometimes the Englishman tries to find a remedy in equality, tries to make of his father a friend. But the friendship is not free: and within it the tie will still chafe him. The Chinaman, instead, makes of his father a god; and that relation, lubricated by the very formality it entails itself, will probably not chafe either of them in the least.

Worship is the smooth, nacreous coating with which the pearl-oyster covers the irritant grain of sand. When any human relationship—parent and child, governor and governed, male and female—seems intolerably fraught with irritation, there is a lot to be said for converting it like this into a *super*human one.

No generalisation however is universal. It is not impossible for a Chinaman to hate his father: only very rare, very rare indeed. When it does happen, because it is so rare it is rendered more arcane, a more potent shaper of the course of his life, than among us. It is something that cannot be breathed aloud: a sacred crime, like incest. Seeing no answering reflection in society around it, the motive is driven down, and inwards: becomes compressed.

Some of the flowers of this hidden root will then be highly curious: and some, even beautiful.

That fireman, Ao Ling, was a young chap—the same age as Dick Watchett: but his had been a more varied career. Not typically Chinese, you might say: there was too much movement in it, too much restless shifting from place to place over big distances. And lately, too much purpose: too little of the happy-go-lucky: a sternness, even an impatience.

A sort of self-oblivion, too, seems to settle on a man, once he has identified himself with a Cause. He will be able to tell you minute details about the Cause itself, from A to Z: but he can hardly tell you whether he himself wears two legs or three.

Ao Ling was in that state now. He had a minute memory of everything which had happened to him up to the time of his conversion, but of very little afterwards. From the time of his conversion, at least down to the time when they fought their way out of Chingkangshan, his mind was a blank, so far as personal things were concerned—it was filled solely with the progress of the Cause. In this ecstasy of religion, small wonder that neither the storm, nor his hunger, nor even the fire from the furnace which had seemed powerless to destroy him, could move him very greatly! Small wonder he had been so bitterly angry at the footling little beliefs of P'ing Tiao.

He sat there in a posture the design of which seemed framed on the bones of his body and the set of his ears, rather than (like most European postures) on the shape of the body's surface. A straight line ran up his spine, up the nape of his neck, up the back of his head. His very short, coarse, thick black hair radiated impartially from a high crown: it was dead-looking, and contrasted surprisingly with his small face, which could be extremely lively and mobile (though it was like a wall, now).

Hunger? For some days now he had been without food. But what are a few days without food to a man who has been through the long faminous siege of Chingkangshan almost without noticing he was hungry?

Hunger had been nothing new to him, even then, in point of fact. For as a child he had once lived through a famine year: and had not forgotten it.

He was seven years old at that time. As his limbs got smaller, his paunch got bigger, so that (like an old man) he could no longer see his knees. From drinking immense quantities of water to fill it, his paunch went hard, and pushed out his little navel till it protruded like a young baby's. He had put nothing solid into that paunch, for five months, but bark and earth—except one day, when the family found a hoard of nine dried beans.

In the earlier months of that winter there had been some food in the house, it is true. But that, naturally, was not given to the children. It was reserved for their grandmother: and the little starvelings used to have to carry her bowl of gruel to her, once a day, with their compliments, until their powers of walking became so uncertain that in common prudence they had to be excused. For one thing which hunger did to them was to take away the power of regular sleeping and waking. Even at night they only slept for a few minutes at a time; and by day they were liable to drop off into a catnap at any moment, whatever they were doing.

There were only two children in the family; Ling and his sister.

One day, late in the famine, they went to the district town, to sell the sister. Most families tried to sell or give away their little girls, those days: but not all were successful. For with so many to choose from the buyers were grown particular. They did not consider it economic to take children under nine years old, being not yet fit for hard work. Those over eleven or twelve, on the other hand, might have wills of their own and make trouble in their new homes: so they too were refused. But Ling's sister was lucky—she was ten, just a good age: ready for hard work, but mentally still dependent. So Ling (who had been unboyishly fond of his *chieh-chieh*) had seen her skinny skull with its sad, monkey eyes, her nobbly elbows and her cracked fingers, for the last time. He saw his father give her: and the buyer, but quite kindly, take her away.

There was a sickening smell everywhere in the town, with so many people dead: and there did not at first seem many of the living about. But as the Ao family threaded the streets on their return home, they came all at once on a large crowd. It was in a street outside the door of a rich man's house. Not the main gate, but a postern, a door of dark polished wood in a perfectly blank wall. Everyone knew the rich man had food in his house: and now the crowd had gathered, without premeditation, in twos and threes, till the street was packed. They did not say much, they just kept up a low growling; though once or twice someone cried out; cursing in falsetto, or supplicating for food. Many were nearly naked. The Aos were soon jammed in the crowd, which still grew: there must have been more than a thousand. Men whom hunger had so withered that their every movement was a gesticulation.

The low whining rose a tone or two, like a storm about to break. If you were impartial you would have feared for that rich man, among his foppish latticed courts and fishponds, with the wolves at last at his door.

The door was opened, from within; and the door-keeper stood there. He was a small, gat-toothed man: but well fed. Alone, the mob surging up to him: but he did not seem afraid of them. He did not speak: but he lifted his hand and pushed the man nearest to him in the chest.

They all went down, falling like a house of cards. In a very short while they were all lying on their backs. Many were too weak to get up again for some time, after the shock of falling: they raised their bodies a little off the ground, weeping with vexation at their own weakness.

Little Ling noticed this collapse of apparently strong men, in the magical face of the Rich, with wonder, and a very curious feeling.

Then the door-keeper closed the door again, hardly bothering to bolt it. Soldiers from the Yamen! There was no need of soldiers, to withstand these autumn leaves.

When they got home, Ao Ling went alone to the little shrine in the fields where the country-gods sat.

In Hazard

Ordinarily they are treated with great respect: given paper clothes, and sniffs of incense, just like the household gods (who, at the New Year, when they repair to Heaven to make their annual report, have their lips smeared with honey that their report may be sweet). But now these were as tattered as their worshippers, their clay bodies as cracked and ill-cared for.

The evening was high-pitched with the shrilling of cicadas: and everywhere the croaking of frogs, like the quacking of a whole fleet of ducks.

Greatly daring, Ling laid hold of the gods: momentarily expecting them to rebuke him. But nothing happened—there was no gate-keeper here!

He dragged them out of the shrine: and with what strength he had, broke them in pieces.

There they lay: powerless to resist, as they had already shown themselves powerless to help: and he started back to the house.

There was a rustling in the dry bamboo-clump. As he passed, in the dusk, something bounded out behind him. It was the god, the fractures showing as fiery seams in his flesh, his green face terrible with anger. Little Ling stumbled screaming into the kitchen, and fell flat on the floor.

All that night he heard the god trampling round the house, or snuffling, for his blood, at the door.

After the famine they moved south, away from the River, into the hills of eastern Hunan: right away from the River.

IV

Why had Ling, among so many filial Chinamen, been one to hate his father? That wrinkled face, with its beard of a few coarse black hairs—why, on the rare occasions he found himself near it, did he always shrink from it, as if he expected a blow?

For their contacts were very rare. In even the poorest, clay-built Chinese house, the women's court (where the children live) is separate from the father's room: an inner place. The only contact the children have with their father is a formal one, when there is some almost ritual act of service to perform. Much as the Chinese love their children, there is no display of affection such as might, in its naked informality, arouse a revulsion in the little one. The pangs of that primeval tie are never allowed to be felt; nor the pearly coating to wear thin.

Ling's father was invariably kind to him, in his remote way: did the right thing by him: dressed him, of course, all in red.

Yet when his father sent him at length to school, because his father sent him he tried not to learn.

However it is difficult not to learn, at a Chinese school. An English boy can stare at a book until he sees double, without reading a word: can shake up the figures of a sum like a kaleidoscope, without coming any nearer the answer. But the Chinese teaching method is subtler. There everything is learned by rote. Say it over and over again: say

In Hazard

it in chorus, for hours and hours. Your attention may be in Tashkent: but say it over and over again like that, in your high piping voice, and it will get in behind your attention: when your attention returns it will be as a lid, not a shield—the thing you wished not to learn will be already safely ensconced within. So too Ao Ling had learned: by rod and by rote, but chiefly by rote.

Yet the impoverished student who conducted the little school could not make much of Ling. He was a polite but a glowering boy, not much liked by his fellows: and with an inner resistance, it almost seemed, to authority. That meant there was no hope for him (for a willing obedience to authority is the first of virtues, without which no others can be added).

Ling's personal hatred of his father, of course, the tutor never suspected. How should he? He was a decent man, not given to the imagination of incredible evil in his pupils. And a feeling so unnatural, so shameful, any child would take pains to hide even from himself. It was only by its fruits that you could tell it was already there.

An exaggerated fear, bordering on a nervous hatred, of the rich, however, the teacher did discern in him: but could not account for.

Only once did the teacher see Ling's face really happy. It was the season of bean-flies—big green insects, with red iridescent eyes. Ling was catching the silly, lovely things in dozens, and putting them

160

in paper boxes: looking at his captives in a most happy and adoring way, holding them with infinite gentleness. The gentle Buddhist himself smiled with pleasure at his student's patent love of them. But then he saw Ling take the boxes, full of living flies, and thrust them, all of a sudden, in the stove.

V

But Ling's early memories went back far beyond those days: beyond his school, beyond the famine: growing even clearer, the earlier they were. Bright separate pictures, recorded not for anything important in them but rather, it seemed, by whim. Almost, Ling believed, he could remember the day when he lay, a new-born babe, wrapped in the traditional pair of his father's old trousers.

That of course is not possible: but some of his memories certainly went back very early indeed.

One was of his sister, of whom he had been so fond. It was in the days before he had learned to walk. He had seen *Chieh-Chieh* toddle out of the door into the sunshine, and on all fours had made haste to follow her. Once out in the yard, he had sat up on his clammy end to look about him. Suddenly he was bowled head over heels by a big, black-haired, wrinkled old boar, who was making a sally at a piece of melon-rind.

In only one of these memories did his father actually make an appearance. I have said that

161

there was little personal contact between them: but in the other picture I propose to describe one of those rare contacts did occur.

The whole family were straddling the thatched roof of their cottage. The yellow flood-water swirled around them, and the mud walls beneath them were melting away. I suppose their peril was pretty acute. Ling was lying in his mother's arms. He must have been very young then: for presently she gave him suck.

However, hardly had the milk begun to come when suddenly his father tore him from her breast, and tossed him, howling furiously, into the rescue-boat which had just drawn near.

Chapter XI

After the famine the Ao family moved south, into the eastern Hunan hills, near the Kiangsi border. By this time Ling's father had grown stern with him: and the boy's hatred deepened. But still he never gave it expression. This was not only a matter of self-control: it was a curious defect in the hatred itself. When alone he might be filled with the white fervour of parricide; but whenever he faced his father a look or a word would prick his rage as if it was a bladder, and leave him humiliated, utterly without its support (acting rather like the push the gate-keeper gave the crowd).

When he was twelve, without warning or any open quarrel, Ling ran away.

He worked here and there, now at this, now at that: being bitten by a restless spirit that made him always move on, from Hunan into Kiangsi, eastward from the wild and wooded hills into the red loam country near Nanchang.

It was on that road he saw his first motor-bus.

163

In Hazard

It was not one of a regular service, but a lone one, far from its fellows, plying wherever a sufficiency of passengers wanted to go. It was packed with passengers so tight that they seemed to spread out at the top like a bunch of flowers: and you could tell by their faces that it was a proud thing to travel by motor-bus.

It was not moving very fast, however, because the proprietor, to economise petrol, had yoked a pair of bullocks to it instead of using the engine.

For a while Ling worked at a country inn, on this road. It had only a few smoke-blackened rooms: one smoky lamp: for general guest-bed a wooden platform. There the few travellers sat peacefully sucking at their little pipes, or relieved their mild boredom by writing and drawing on the walls. The shrill mosquitoes: the crowing cocks: the midnight stamping of the cattle: and at dawn the rattling chain by which he drew water from the well.

What a contrast it was to the urban hotel (where presently he got another job) in Nanchang!—Nanchang, the first capital town he set eyes on, and therefore the world's metropolis to him. The singsong of the peddlers in the street: the clatter, the strident singing, the everlasting shapeless noise: the smell of bean-oil: the snapping voices of men gambling, for drinks, all night with their fingers: the soldiers roused at bugle-crow, and the sewing-machines.

164

Saturday

Sitting in the centre-castle of the "Archimedes," Ao Ling closed his ears to the Christian buffoon: let his reverie course over the chequered field of his memories.

For a time he had worked as a navvy, repairing the dykes that hold the yellow Yangtze back from the green land behind.

For a time he had worked in a Shanghai theatre. Not as an actor, nor property-man, nor musician, nor any job you would think of with the word "theatre" in your mind. In that baking heat, his job was to toss among the audience hot towels, with which to ease their congested sweat-glands.

—Again, a time in Nanking: where they had already begun to raise a new, gaunt Whitehall in the earthen ruins.

A time when he had stood, his arms bound behind him, waiting his turn to kneel before the headsman. It was a sandy space, like a football-ground, outside a city wall: and surrounded by a football crowd. But even as he waited his turn someone galloped up with news, shouting. The headsman (one of the last of his guild), his smug and vain expression turned suddenly to terror, dropped his cleaver and ran, his yellow apron flapping against his knees. The punctilious Magistrate, presiding in his bivouac of matting, vanished without punctilio. The soldiers ran: the crowd melted: he was left alone, one living man among four decapitated bodies, the cold sweat drying on his stiffened and aching face.

His hands were still tied behind him as he wandered into the emptying town. A silent town: no voice raised in alarm, only a whispering all over it like a shower of rain—the whisper of running feet. When he had found something to cut himself free he ran too.

Not long after that he spent a merry three months as conductor on the Hangchow bus: a most light-hearted, boyish time. These were proper buses, proceeding under their own power. Back and forth to Nanking, for three months, always through the same countryside. It is a delicate, detailed, green country—all shades of green, green rice-fields, dark green corn-fields, green trees, green feathery clumps of bamboo. A country of earthen roads, and hump-backed bridges over canals thick with quiet, child-drawn traffic. Over these roads the bulging and intoxicated buses roared and raced; each with its wildly-swaying luggage-trailer like a tin can tied to a bolting terrier's tail.

In this job Ling developed a passion for machinery, and in time might even have risen to the rank of driver. But one day, as they bucketed over a bridge with all their wheels in the air, he caught a glimpse of a beautiful boat-girl, sitting in a sampan and embroidering slippers. Hers was a beauty that would have made even a wild goose alight.

166

Without hesitation he dropped off the moving bus.

But by the time he had run back to the bridge, the sampan was gone.

Actually Ao Ling was back in Hunan, a soldier in the army of General Ho Chien, at the time of his conversion.

That was in 1927. All Hunan and Kiangsi were in a turmoil. The Northern troops had come and gone: but now a new sort of warfare had begun. For no sooner was the Kuomintang safely in the ascendant than it split from top to bottom—Right from Left. Borodin and the Russians were sent packing. Communists, big and little, were slaughtered wherever they could be caught. For no one is so merciless to the Left as the old revolutionary: and chronologically it was Chiang Kai-shek's government at Nanking, not the Nazi government of Hitler, which can claim the honour of being the second of the world's fascist movements (Stalin of course only comes fourth).

Yet some of the leading Communists escaped the proscription; and raising their standard here and there, found no lack of adherents. Mao Tse-tung, for instance: a slatternly peasant-politician of thirty, with an educated and humorous mind. And Chu Teh: a comfortably-off, aristocratic, middle-aged, opium-smoking Brigadier-general, who had renounced everything to kiss the Hammer and

167

Sickle: and who was a strategist, moreover, of the first class.

Mao, working from Changsha (the provincial capital) roused the peasants of Hunan to revolt; and presently marched south with them to the mountains of the Kiangsi border. The reformed Chu Teh, who had led his troops with him out of Nanchang, marched west, into these same mountains.

So this brilliant and incongruous pair joined forces, and established themselves first in Chingkangshan.

But of all this, of course, Ao Ling knew little at that time. Only that Old Sly-boots His Excellency Ho Chien was sending the force to which he belonged into the mountains, to fight the "bandits."*
Those mountains, that he already knew so well. Old Sly-boots was an efficient commander, whose troops went where he told them. And so, shouldering their umbrellas, their huge straw hats flapping on their backs, some carrying song-birds in cages,

---

* The government made a practice of referring to the Communist forces as "bandits." But the word has not quite the same connotation as in English. The Chinese bandit does not operate solely for gain: the game, for that alone, would not be worth the candle. He is often moved by a strong moral principle as well. Banditry (before the appearance of Communism in China) used to absorb what in Europe would have become revolutionary elements. But it is characteristic that where the European revolutionary is out to overthrow the social system, the Chinese bandit only repairs it: for economically, he serves the useful purpose of keeping wealth circulating. When caught he is, of course, executed.

and a few even carrying rifles, the Government forces moved to the attack.

That was the point at which Ao Ling's mind went blank, so far as his own experiences were concerned. How had he found himself in the ranks of that Red Army he had been sent to fight? He hardly knew. There were plenty of other deserters, like himself: they went over in small groups, all the time—as they had always been accustomed to do, in these local wars. Ling must have gone with a group like that: perhaps even guided them.

He had certainly no notion, as he trotted across to the enemy lines, that this was the beginning of a new life for him: that it was more than a change of leaders: that it would come to mean, to him, what the Road to Damascus meant to St. Paul.

Yet that is what happened. He absorbed the Marxist doctrine like a thirsty animal drinking. It refreshed every corner of his soul. For it freed him from his three great fears: fear of his father, fear of the supernatural, fear of the rich. Moreover it harnessed the three hatreds born of those fears, and told him they were proper and right—not the secret scars of a wandering outcast, but the honourable badges of a fraternity. In setting him to fight the government it made his father hydra-headed—and gave him a sword for every neck.

He remembered the old life clearly, but it meant nothing to him any more—almost it might have

169

happened to someone else. Like those memories of an earlier life on earth which a re-incarnate might preserve, who had somehow avoided Mother Mêng's potion of oblivion.

Ling, who had never been able to work even for himself for more than a few months at a time, now found himself prepared to work his whole life for the sake of the New China: for the dawn of the Red Star. He developed a great natural aptitude for learning, which he had never guessed he had in him: gulping books and lectures with an almost appalling voracity: and presently, delivering passable lectures himself.

But it was not so much his book-learning that first brought him into public notice as the almost uncanny skill he developed at ping-pong; a craze for which was then already sweeping the entire Red Higher Command like a fever.

II

All that winter they were beleaguered in Ching-kangshan: and once again Ao Ling tasted bark soup. But in the spring of '29 the Red Army burst its bounds: fought its way out of the ring surrounding it and went off campaigning and preaching in southern Kiangsi. But in the sortie, the patrol which Ao Ling now commanded got separated from the Army: and presently Ao Ling got separated from his patrol. He was suddenly alone.

The effect on him was immediate and terrifying:

he felt himself shrinking, shrivelling. All that winter he had been not a person, but a unit in a great fraternity, all members of one body. Now he was alone. He was no longer a patrol-commander, working his way, according to Hoyle, down the Western System of Defiles: he was a lonely man with a stubbed toe, hobbling down a steep, stone-flagged path: approaching through a clump of firs a little Taoist temple, on the walls of which huge anti-communist posters flamed. Before the door the abbot sat, playing on a zither.

Up in the mountains he had been wallowing for six months in the life of the spirit, in communion. But now the illusion of the Red-Dust was on him again: once more the visible world existed. He became again clearly conscious of the familiar country round him: the tree-capped crags, the little verdant valleys. The smoke rising from the grey villages. The comfortable country-houses, black and white timber-and-plaster beneath their curly eaves. The deeply-lowing, reddish cattle. A pathetic donkey with a weight tied to its tail, so that it might not lift it—and being unable to lift it, might not bray.

The Red Army was God-knows-where—certainly it had not passed that way. He could rejoin it later. The first thing for Ao Ling to do, a communist and a deserter from Ho Chien's army, was to get out of the Province of Hunan.

As if he were aware of the stranger's thoughts,

171

the abbot laid down his zither and remarked placidly:

"When a tiger is expected in the path, it is foolish to remain and tickle its nostrils with a straw."

"I wash my ears, Old Immortal, and listen with reverence," Ao Ling replied—forgetting, for the moment, his anti-clericalism.

The sun showed him which was the south; and so at a steady trot, in spite of his stubbed toe, he set out for the borders of Kwangtung. It took him five days to reach an escarpment from which he could see, below, the Pei river running through the tufted pinnacles of rock which line its bed. On the Pei river he took passage, unknown, in a boat for Canton.

But Canton, even, was no place for a known Communist: the proscription still raged. It was impossible to rejoin the Red Army—for its whereabouts were too uncertain. So Ao Ling put himself at the disposal of the Party: and the Party provided him with a set of genuine-looking seaman's papers. With their aid he was signed on the "Archimedes," then lying at Hongkong.

III

It was no part of the contract, when the Party by a stroke of the pen converted Ao Ling into a Fireman of three years' standing, that he should spread communism among the crew of the "Archimedes." The time for action of that kind was not

172

ripe: there was little to gain by a few abortive mutinies. They had enough on their hands already, with the forces of the Kuomintang to resist, without exasperating the Powers into giving those forces more aid than they were giving already.

Ao Ling did not even carry with him any Marxist texts, for private devotion: the risk of discovery was too great. Consequently he was able to give the whole force of his new-found powers of learning to his old passion for machinery. There would be need, he knew very well, some day in the New China of men who could tend machines with skill. The raw material of engineers is rarer than the raw material of political martyrs.

And yet, at this moment, he was tempted very sorely. He knew that though these seamen were now sitting harmlessly listening to the story-teller, it would not be difficult to turn their minds to serious things. Being by nature stubbornly slaves, they would under ordinary conditions have been hard to rouse against the Imperialists: but this was a special moment, which would pass, and perhaps not return. Their heavy minds were now light with hunger and terror: easily swayed.

He felt a sudden conviction of power, surging into his finger-tips. He could stand up and speak: make these men follow him. They could overpower the officers, seize the ship. You can see that the temptation would be terrific, to a man who had never before been able to do anything effective

173

on his own. At the thought of this God-the-Father of a Captain, reduced to an ordinary man—naked, but for his clothes—Ao Ling felt his muscles tremble, and a momentary flash of red light seemed to come out of the lantern.

Yes, he could do it.

But he had not the right. To act on his own, contrary to the express orders of the Party, was to be the worst sort of traitor. Duty utterly forbade it.

But was it only duty which made him open his fist, as it were, and let the opportunity slip through it? Or was it an older compulsion? At least, the feeling of collapse, as the erectile power in him ebbed and seemed to run out through the soles of his feet, was itself no new sensation to Ao Ling.

Henry Tung was telling them how he had dined once with some Taoists. As it grew dark, they had no lantern: so the eldest priest cut a moon out of white paper, and pinned it on the wall: where it hung, and flooded the whole room with light. It was certainly the real moon: for if you looked carefully you could see Hêng O herself, the Moon-Fairy, sitting there among the cinnamon-groves; her jade-white hare at her side. Presently the whole party stepped up into the moon—Henry and all, he said—to take a drink with the lady. But it was too cold, in those frozen horizons, to stop there long.

"I can cap that!" said Ao Ling suddenly: and

174

burst forth into the most extraordinary story of a thing that had happened, he said, at the country inn at which he once worked. Two travellers had been sitting late over their supper, when they saw a girl's head poking through the wall and laughing at them. One of the travellers jumped up: but the head withdrew, leaving the wall as before. This happened several times. So he grew angry: and drawing a knife, crept on hands and knees to the foot of the wall, and waited. Presently the head popped through again, and he slashed up at the white throat with all his might. He cut the head clean off: it rolled on the floor all bloody:

"Loud cries! The landlord rushed in. There was the knife. The bleeding head still blinked its eyes. But wonder! There was no hole in the wall! No mark upon it! No body!—The men were arrested: but no body was ever found. . . ."

"*All man listen my talkee!*" said a startling, clear voice.

Every eye turned towards where the pin-point of an electric torch was aimed at them. Behind it, they could just see the Captain: and with him, Mr. Soutar and Mr. Watchett. He stepped forward into the lantern-light, an officer at each shoulder. Mr. Soutar was making signs: trying to point out Henry Tung to him.

"Sea too much bobbery? No can catchee chow-chow, heh?" he began, and took their silence for

175

agreement. Then he went on to point the moral: "I makee my pidgin, you makee your pidgin, good Joss! Ship can reach port! All man work hard can catchee cumshaw!"

"Cumshaw" means "bonus." Instantly before each brightening inward eye silver dollars danced on a wooden desk.

He paused for a moment, before advancing the second side of his argument, and put his hand into his pocket.

"—Suppose you makee trouble? My got irons. You no forget my got *this* piecee!" He brought his hand out suddenly, with a revolver in it. "My no wantchee bobbery!"

He paused again, to let the position sink in: for it had better, before he came to the third phase of the matter. Then suddenly he burst out in a trumpeting sternness:

"My plenty savvy have got this place one piecee bad man! No belong sailorman, belong pilate man! *Velly* bad man! Velly bad joss!"

Suddenly he spun round, pointing his revolver at Ao Ling.

"Arrest that man, Mr. Watchett," he said.

Dick sprang forward with alacrity—with far too much, being unused to making an arrest: and almost tumbled on top of Ao Ling. All the faces of the crew were turned towards them, like surprised moons, and Mr. Soutar spluttered, "But . . . but . . ."

Dick seized one wrist; fumbled with the hand-cuffs, and dropped them. Ao Ling, terrified, put up his other hand to shield his face. Dick, surprised at the sinewy strength of the wrist he held, and thinking the other meant a blow, clenched his fist and drove hard at Ao Ling's cheek. The sinewy wrist relaxed, limp as a girl's: Ao Ling fell back, and Dick handcuffed him as he lay.

"I've known about this man for a long time, Mr. Soutar," the Captain said in an aside: "He came on board at Hongkong with forged papers. I got a wireless from the Hongkong police, asking me to arrest him. He's a well-known bandit, by what they say."

"You've known it a long time, Sir?"

"Yes; but I had not meant to make the arrest till we got to port. But now you come and tell me trouble is brewing: seemed a good chance. You saw for yourself he was the real ring-leader, he was haranguing them nineteen to the dozen. I don't think there will be any trouble after this—your Master Henry will pipe down."

He turned again to the Chinese.

"That man belong plenty bad man! You have look-see what fashion my makee with bad man: my catchee him takee lock-up. *You* good man, you no fear. Makee your pidgin, obey order chop-chop, good joss! Bymeby can come port pay plenty cumshaw: pay all man two dollar!"

Most of his hearers smiled. They were not much

177

concerned about Ao Ling: what they were concerned about was getting justice for themselves. Well, they were to have it: a cumshaw (bonus) was justice. Two dollars a cataclysm: that was ample justice.

Captain Edwardes's conscience, however, was not too comfortable. His behaviour he felt, had not been as scrupulous as he liked it to be towards Chinese. And yet, if Mr. Soutar was right, surely the coup was justified. As for young Watchett's bungling and violence, Captain Edwardes felt deeply to blame for it.

Ao Ling was handcuffed now: but he was still knocked out. They could not wait for him to revive: too much of an anti-climax. So Dick, blushing rather ashamedly at the unnecessary force he had used, bent to pick the man up.

He was astonished at the softness, now, of the limp body in his arms: the smoothness of the skin: and his shame grew. Ao Ling hanging limp like that in his arms, was almost as light as Sukie had been.

Mr. Soutar helping him, he carried Ao Ling to the Hospital (as a convenient cell for the moment): laid him more gently on the bed than a policeman should: and locked him in.

Chapter XII

It seemed Captain Edwardes was a good judge of "Joss": or else he had looked at the barometer. Anyhow, the barometer had already risen at the time he arrested Ao Ling, and it continued to rise all the night, and with dawn the wind noticeably slackened. By nine o'clock it was certain and plain, that the sucking of the storm had relaxed its hold on them: that they were at last spewed out. I do not mean that the storm was over, it continued on its course with equal fury: but the "Archimedes" was no longer in it. She had fallen out of the back.

The wind was no more, now, than a strong breeze—a yachtsman's gale. The ship lay with her nose generally north-east, and what wind there was varied from south-west to west—was almost directly aft.

Everybody knows that a boat under sail does not roll as badly as a motor-boat. The wind holds

179

on to the sail; and steadies her, whatever the waves may be up to. But should a sudden calm drop, while the sea is still rough, she will roll till your teeth rattle. Something of the same sort happened now. While the hurricane lasted the "Archimedes" had been pinned down almost as if her slab sides were working-canvas: the seas could not do with her altogether according to their whim. But now that the steadying hurricane was relaxed, there was nothing to restrain her motion: she danced like a frenzied cork, she rolled as she had never rolled since the weather began. What little on board of her had not smashed before, smashed now. The few remaining life-boats kicked out their chocks, and with broken backs somersaulted in their falls: the saloon table, bolted to the deck, snapped off its own legs. There was an unmusical clanging everywhere like abominable bells. Wire guys parted; or, with a small remnant of their object weighting the loose end, cracked like whips. Looked on as a pandemonium, the ship was worse than she had ever been.

Moreover the seas were coming up astern, pooping her. No one could have done any oiling now in the after latrines, they were spouting like geysers. The bulkheads of the after-castle were being stove in, one after another: water was pouring over the steering engine. The seas began to come clean over the after-castle, their weight levering the forward end of the ship sometimes right out of the water. When they did that, of course, much of the water went down the gap in No. 6 hatch: reducing that perilous margin very fast.

Dick Watchett could hardly believe his senses, when he found that the wind had dropped, and the risen barometer proved that this was no "centre" again, but at last the storm's periphery. He hurried to the Bridge—to get the good news confirmed. He found the Captain and Mr. Buxton in the chartroom, both holding on to the built-in chart-roller.

"Is it true, Sir?" he burst out: "Are we really out of the storm?"

Captain Edwardes nodded. And then, looking at the Captain's face, Dick saw an astonishing thing. Captain Edwardes was, for the first time in that storm, afraid.

Dick looked back at the ship beneath him: and saw why. He saw the poop disappear in a shifting tumble of foam that raced forward right to the very centre-castle. She winced under it; her bows, even viewed from the height of the Bridge, mounting almost to the horizon. It passed; but her stern did not very greatly rise. Without doubt she was now down by the stern.

Just at that moment Sparks appeared on the Bridge, to report his emergency set was once more working.

"Send a call to all ships," said Captain Edwardes:

In Hazard

"Estimated position so-and-so, require immediate assistance! And keep on sending."

Sparks, with blanched face, departed on his ominous duty.

But it is not much use sending out a call for urgent help unless you know your actual position pretty certainly. There are methods by which other vessels can get a rough idea of your direction: but even then they may have a long search before they find you.

The estimated position Captain Edwardes sent out was plainly very wrong, by the messages that presently came pouring in—from vessels near that position, who found no "Archimedes," nor even weather like hers.

If they had to make a prolonged search, help would arrive too late. For if the "Archimedes" was going down, she would do it quickly.

But if she did not sink in the next hour or so, with the wind gone the sea must presently moderate. Then she would be comparatively safe.

But still the sky was obscured: no chance of a sight of the sun, to tell him where he was.

One message that came was relayed from Boston—it was from his Owners, in Bristol:

"Master Archimedes. Salvage vessel Patricia been searching you three days stop are you sinking condition query Endeavour utmost to ascertain your true position stop Sage."

Captain Edwardes, his brown eyes staring

brightly and his lower lip drawn over his teeth, seemed suddenly moved by determination and a kind of anger. He fished out a sodden wireless form from his pocket, dented it laboriously with a stubby blacklead:

"*Sage, Bristol. Hurriçane moderating. Am confident of safety of ship will proceed Kingston. Edwardes.*"

He pushed the original and his reply under Mr. Buxton's nose.

The latter whistled faintly through a hollow tooth.

"Will proceed?" he said.

"Will proceed," answered the captain.

Captain Edwardes blew a double blast on his whistle, and a little quartermaster came padding along.

"Ask Mr. MacDonald to step on the Bridge."

Presently the Chief Engineer appeared: his eyes wild and bleary, his false teeth in his hand.

"Mr. MacDonald, what is it prevents you getting steam on the Donkey?"

"Nae funne'."

"Well, the wind has moderated now. What's to prevent you rigging a jury-funnel? I want enough steam for the pumps in two hours. Can you do it?"

"A canna," said Mr. MacDonald: "Bu' A can 'ry."

So the engineers broke off one of the few tall, hooded ventilators that had remained unsmashed:

183

and with the help of some cement stepped it on the stump of the old donkey-funnel: they guyed it very firmly with wire guys (which was very clever in that motion): then went inside again to try to light the donkey-furnace.

Four hours, not two, had passed when they had reluctantly to admit it was still no go. Even with a jury-funnel, the hot oil still ran out of the furnace door.

Captain Edwardes set his teeth, his bright eyes seeming concentrated on the problem of the present: but in reality his mind was travelling back into the past. His own past, before he joined the Sage Line: when he was still in Sail. For like every other senior officer in the fleet, his training had been in Sail, not Steam. It is only lately, when the supply of sail-trained officers has begun to run short, that most of the first-class steamship lines have begun to accept officers trained in Steam alone: have begun to train such officers themselves.

This seems an anomaly, to landsmen: that steamship companies should actually require their officers to have been trained in sail: landsmen are inclined to smile, as at a piece of foolish conservatism—as if London Bus-drivers were required to serve for seven years as stable-boys and grooms, before they were allowed to handle motor-buses. With so much technical knowledge to acquire anyhow, why waste the man's time in learning a useless and outmoded technique as well?

The answer is a matter of Virtue, really. For an inclination towards virtue (such as sent Mr. Buxton to sea) is not enough in itself; it must be trained, like any other aptitude. Now there is a fundamental difference in kind between the everyday work of a sailing-vessel and the everyday work of a steamer. The latter does not essentially differ from a shore job: it is only occasionally, rarely, that emergencies arise in Steam. But every common action in the working of a sailing-vessel, all the time, partakes of something of the nature of an emergency. Everything must be done with your whole heart, and a little more than your whole strength. Thus is a natural aptitude for virtue increased by everyday practice. For changing a jib in a stiff breeze is a microcosm, as it were, of saving the ship in a storm.

So the officer in Sail acquires a training in virtue that may later, in Steam, mean the saving of some hundred lives, and a million or so of property.

If this had been a sailing-ship, Captain Edwardes reflected, now something could have been done. Jury-masts rigged, jury sails bent, so she could escape out of the seething of this hell-broth. But what can you do in a steamer?

He remembered one of his early voyages, in a little Portmadoc schooner of a hundred and fifty tons. They were dismasted in a North Sea gale, fastened themselves below and rolled helpless as the "Archimedes" now rolled. They were bringing

185

home a cargo of timber; the holds were packed tight with it, and their decks had been piled high with it too till the storm washed those decks as clean as a brass door-plate. Presently she had rolled clean over—and up the other side. I know it sounds incredible—but that is what happened. For proof, there were the burns on the cabin ceiling, where hot cinders from the cabin stove had fallen on it! (But if the "Archimedes" rolled over like that, she would not come up again before the Day of Judgment.)

Once the storm relaxed, captain and crew of the schooner had reappeared—like head and legs out of a re-assured tortoise. Her masts were gone: but they had plenty of timber below decks, with which they built up small masts, and stepped them in the pumps. She would not come to windward under this improvised rig: but she made a port to leeward without too much difficulty. No salvage-ship was sent combing the seas for *her*!

And then Captain Edwardes recalled his first voyage as a steamship officer. On watch on the bridge, he had seen a squall coming. In a sailing vessel, there would have been plenty for the officer of the watch to do. But what do you do on a steamer, when you see a squall coming? Nothing, except stroll into the wheel-house to shelter from the rain.

It cuts both ways. The knight in armour could laugh at the slings and stones of the footboys. But once he fell off his horse, there he stayed—he could not even stand up again on his feet without help. The steamship officer can laugh at squalls, and contrary winds. But once he is in a real hole, there he stops.

And yet, surely something could be done. For a moment Edwardes had a mad idea of putting the "Archimedes" also under jury-rig: sailing her to safety. Bend awnings to her few remaining derricks. But all the awnings were cut up, for hatch-covers. And again, without steam how could he shift the bloody rudder? It is no good sailing if you cannot steer.

Well, they could rig tackles on the rudder-head: and perhaps all heaving together they could shift the rudder, in time. But that is not steering: why, it might take ten minutes to shift the rudder a few degrees.

Still, perhaps it might be done . . . and at least the sails might stop her rolling like this. . . .

Again he remembered that his awnings were all cut up, now, for hatch-covers: there was nothing to make sails out of.

If they were ever to move again, it must be by steam. And the oil would not burn.

After all, she was a *steamer:* everything in her depended on steam. You could not carry her back into the days of sail, not effectively. If you improvised anything, it must be a way to raise steam you improvised.

187

In Hazard

In short, if the oil would not burn they must burn something else.

Captain Edwardes sought out Mr. MacDonald, and found him staring at the still dribbling donkey.

"Mr. MacDonald," he said: "what about solid fuel?"

"Aye, gin we had coal, an' fire-bars. But we ha'e nae coal, let be fire-bars."

"Wood?"

Mr. MacDonald looked at the captain for a moment as if the latter had gone insane: then he gave his thigh a great slap.

At first sight it would appear as difficult to burn solid fuel in an oil-furnace as to stoke up your gas-ring with lumps of charcoal. But it is not so bad, really. The chief thing you need is fire-bars, for the fuel to rest on. Some ships (though not many nowadays) actually have convertible furnaces, and carry fire-bars so that they can change over from oil to coal fuel if necessary or convenient. The "Archimedes" did not: but all the same, fire-bars could surely be improvised.

So Mr. MacDonald set the engineers to work on a new task: they collected a number of super-heat elements (these are fasces of thin tubes, four or five together) and with hack-saws cut them off to the length of the furnaces, supporting them on fire-bricks. The short ends they laid over them cross-wise. Then the furnaces were stuffed with dunnage and broken furniture, and they were fired.

By the time they came to fix the bars her motion must have been noticeably easier: or they would never have succeeded in doing it.

II

Indeed it was certainly easier, that afternoon: and Captain Edwardes began to believe that the confidence which he had expressed but not felt had been after all justified. The pooping was rarer: until at last it was possible to cover No. 6 hatch properly. After that, no more water went below. But she must have eleven hundred tons in her at least, by now: she was listed at 35° and down by the stern: head up and only one ear cocked, as it were. The position was still critical.

Now that the danger seemed somewhat relaxed, and the incessant buffeting was over, the famishment of everyone became very serious. Dick took to walking about in a slightly bent position so as to ease his emptiness. Then the First Officer suggested that it might be possible, now her motion was eased, to get something at last out of the flooded store-room. The store-room was right forward, under the fo'c'sle. No one could possibly have entered it while her motion was still fierce, even during a lull.

The ladder down into the store-room had broken loose, broken a hole in the floor, broken itself, and disappeared. Beneath the floor were bags of rice:

189

and swelling in all that sea water they had burst the whole floor up, and then begun to ferment horribly. If they had had time, they would have made it impossible to enter the store-room at all without a gas mask; but they had only just begun fermenting now. So Dick was lowered down, sitting in the bight of a rope, with an iron hook in his hand. It was a dizzy business: he swung on his rope one way, while the water beneath him sloshed the other way. So he, and the cans and cases he was trying to grapple, rushed about with great violence in many directions, but (like two relatives who have arranged to meet in a huge crowd) never seemed able to collide.

At last however he managed to grapple two cases, and they were pulled up. One was a case of Bass, the other of tinned peaches. Then he was hauled up himself—half unconscious, what with the swinging and the gases from the rice.

The Chief Steward, of course, was at hand to receive the stores: and at once he issued the canned peaches. But he would not allow one single bottle of the Bass to be opened, till he had found his book of chits. He did not like irregularity of any kind.

When the cans of peaches were first opened, the glands in their jaws hurt excruciatingly at the sight. For this was Sunday: and they had only had one other snack since Thursday morning: no proper meal for nearly a week.

III

By now the engineers were beginning to cry out for more wood. There was no dry wood to be had, of course: but apparently once the centre donkey furnace was going they could dry wood sufficiently by it to light the other two. The thing was now that they must have quantities of wood: for the furnaces had to be kept roaring if they were to raise any steam, and wood burnt away in no time. So everyone was kept running hither and thither for more. It was like trying to get a kettle to boil, at a picnic, with only bits of paper to burn. There was plenty of spoilt stuff of all kinds on the "Archimedes," from packing cases in the holds to the saloon furniture: the only job was to break it up and to bring it up to the donkey-room fast enough. So all the officers hacked with axes, breaking and splitting and busting, and all the Chinamen ran with bundles of faggots—earning their blessed "cumshaws."

It is wonderful how the free busting of anything, especially valuable stuff, goes to your head. Dick grinned with pleasure as he cleft bunks into faggots. Even Mr. Buxton grinned as he chopped at the broken mahogany turned legs of the saloon table. The Chinamen, carrying the stuff, wore broad grins. Mr. Rabb, now working as hard as anyone, was the only one who did not grin: but his axe fell with the unerring skill, and the force, of personal enmity.

191

In Hazard

Soon the donkey-room, and all spaces near it, were piled high with wood like a junk-yard. And the engineers everlastingly stoked like devils. They would have to keep it up all night, though, if they were to raise the steam to any usable pressure.

IV

Dick was on watch, that night, from twelve till four. As he climbed the bridge he noticed a change in the air: a softness. Rain still fell in showers: but they pattered on your face delicately, refreshingly, instead of lashing your skin like dog-whips. Being (like them all) very deaf, the quiet seemed to him unnatural. The sea now had settled down to a steady, very long swell.

All was dark, except where a glow showed from the donkey-room: occasionally broken by a dark figure passing in or out. The stoking, the carrying of wood still went on.

Visibility was not very good: the night seemed very dark, the clouds low and close, so that you could not tell the level of the horizon at all: a warm, moist, woolly night.

Suddenly the heavens opened, and a patch of brilliant starlit sky appeared. At the same time the horizon showed, stark and clear. After so long in the dark, the stars seemed to shine with an almost blinding, icy fire. Dick caught his breath in wonder: then made a dash to the chartroom to get out his sextant.

Chapter XIII

After a long period without sleep, a healthy young man likes to make it up by sleeping for fourteen hours or so at a stretch. But the routine of watch-keeping makes this impossible on a ship.

The older men, after five days and nights without sleep, found it very difficult to sleep at all. Captain Edwardes still did not yet feel himself nap on his cabin sofa. Mr. MacDonald, on the other hand, made no attempt to sleep—he knew it would be hopeless. He walked about ceaselessly, talking chiefly about Chinamen and water (though not saying anything very sensible about either). The younger men, on the other hand (such as Gaston and Dick Watchett) once they were asleep found waking after a few hours an agony: they were dragged back to consciousness as miserably as a partially-drowned man is restored—wishing they had never slept at all, rather than that they should have been dragged back like that.

When a man is in that state, it is hard to say

exactly when he does wake. Certainly not when he first answers you, in his bunk, in crisp tones but with his eyes closed, and not moving. Is it when he jumps out on to the floor, and, his eyes still shut, feels about for his boots? Or perhaps after he has been going about his duties for a quarter of an hour?

Dick certainly had no memory of getting out of his bunk that morning. The first thing he could remember was when he was on deck. It was a limpid and lovely morning. The sea was smooth, except for a slight, very long, very rapid swell, that passed almost faster than the eye could follow it, and gave the ship no time to rise and fall. The sky was the blue of a field of gentians: the air clear as glass, but warm: the very sea seemed washed, it sparkled so blue, so diamond-bright. The blue wood-smoke from the improvised donkey-funnel floated up into the still air, and hung there, the only cloud there was, scenting all the horrible litter of the decks with its sweet smell. It was such a morning that you could hardly believe no larks would presently rise, ascending on their clear voices into the clear sky.

The voices of the woodmen in the donkey-room rose sharp but still faint; and the occasional blow of an axe.

Dick heard an order given, in a confident voice. There was a hiss, as steam-cocks were turned on: then the sudden clanging of the pumps: loud at

194

first till the water began to rise: then steady, and slow. They were pumping out No. 6 hold. A brown and filthy stream, creamy with air-bubbles, began to cascade into the clean sea.

The pool of brown in the clear blue spread. Presently Dick noticed a queer thing: fish rising to the surface of it, floating dead, their white bellies up. It was so impregnated with tobacco juice, it poisoned any fish who came near it. Imagine all that nicotine, flowing through delicate gills!

The pumps could not work for long at a time: the highest pressure of steam the wood-furnaces could raise was forty pounds (roughly, the pressure in a motor-tyre): and they could not hold it long. A brief spell of work: and then a rest, while they stoked the furnace once more. Meanwhile, the brown stain in the sea faded to a yellow opaqueness. But the poisoned fish remained, floating round the "Archimedes" in hundreds, with starting eyes and fixed, gaping mouths.

Presently the pumps began their painful and poisonous vomiting once more.

It may have killed the fish, but it put wonderful new heart into the crew of the "Archimedes": and as the level of water in the after holds fell they sang, and worked like blazes. In their zeal they smashed for firewood even objects that were not really seriously damaged. For there were a few of these, after all, saved in a miraculous way. The book-case in the smoking room, for instance: a flimsy affair with a glass front. It had fallen on its face on the floor, and in some unaccountable way not even the glass was broken. Yet a saloon table, I told you, had been snapped off its clamped legs. It was not as if the book-case contained a Bible—you could not even find a superstitious reason for its being saved. It only contained ordinary literature.

Another pretty miraculous thing, when you come to think of it, was that nobody had been killed. Things had been happening all round them as lethal as an air-raid: yet there were no casualties. Not even a broken bone. Everyone, nearly, was cut and bruised, but that was all. The worst sufferer was Mr. Soutar: at one moment the heaviest midshipman had been flung onto a particularly bad bunion he had; and he had yelled with agony. He limped from it still.

II

By sight of a star at dawn, and a solar sight later, Captain Edwardes was at last able to fix his position. Being so far from his estimated position, the calculation took him some time. And when he plotted the result on the chart, he rubbed his eyes. He was away a hundred miles north of Cape Gracias: all banks passed. The storm had carried him nearly four hundred miles from the point at which it had struck him: in five days. Moreover it had probably not taken him direct there: curving, they had probably drifted at least a hundred miles

196

a day. An average speed of four knots—travelled, for the most part, broadside on. Of course, a speed through the water of four knots, broadside on, was hardly possible. The storm must have carried the sea along with it too. And indeed, when he examined the chart, he saw that his earlier surmise must have been true: that the sea was raised up, near the centre of the storm, in a flattish cone, with a circular motion (only slower) like that of the wind: and so they had passed safely over banks they could never have crossed if the sea had been at its normal level!

The first thing he did, of course, when he found his position was to announce it to the "Patricia": and when he got her reply, he was thankful. For this steam raised on wood—it was after all only make-believe. It enabled them to do a bit of pumping: or when in tow, perhaps it would work the steering-gear. It could work the fans: but he knew very well the fans alone could never get the main furnaces going, from cold, without a main funnel. It could never really enable them to raise main steam again.

Nevertheless, it had served two useful purposes. Most of them knew that yesterday, the day the storm had abandoned them, had been the most dangerous day of all. For six hours at least the ship might have sunk any minute. Without hard and hopeful work could these worn men have borne the strain? That was one thing: and there was another. They would presently have to be taken in tow by the salvage vessel: and the salvage the Owners would have to pay would in any case be very heavy. But salvage is proportional to the helplessness of the vessel salved. Captain Edwardes might save them a lot off the award, if the "Archimedes" had at least auxiliary steam on her.

Meanwhile the engineers continued pumping: and the Deck set about a new task. They borrowed a little steam for a winch, to haul some hawsers up on deck. They were preparing a tow-rope. For by now they were in constant communication with the "Patricia": already acting largely under her orders. And to all other offers of assistance a general reply was sent: thanks, but it was not needed.

It was at one that midday that the "Patricia" was sighted. First, her smoke above the horizon. Thereupon (since the "Archimedes's" little whiff would hardly be visible to her) Edwardes wirelessed his bearing to her: and she was soon close.

She looked like a small black steamer, rather than a tug.

She steamed right round the "Archimedes," taking a good look at her. Well she might! I doubt if she had ever seen a vessel looking like the "Archimedes" floating the sea. You see vessels like the "Archimedes" lying up on a reef somewhere, sometimes: but you do not see them floating on the sea.

Then she stopped, and lowered a boat. Sixteen men climbed into it, and rowed across. It was a romantic sight, these sixteen men coming to the rescue of the stricken vessel. Captain Edwardes on the bridge counted them—sixteen. And Dick also counted them, as he stood at the rail, waiting to lower a pilot-ladder to them (for both gangways were gone). *Sixteen.*

Sixteen men! Captain Edwardes was almost too shaken to speak. "Mr. Buxton," he said, "stand by that pilot-ladder and allow no man on board but the master only."

Buxton picked up a thick piece of wood: gave another to Dick:

"If anyone but the master tries to board us, club him back into the sea!"

Other officers joined them.

Captain Abraham was standing in the boat's sternsheets: his bow-man laid hold of the ladder.

"Keep your men in the boat, Captain," roared Edwardes from the bridge. "I allow no man on board but yourself!"

"What the hell, Captain," Captain Abraham began: "I insist . . ."

Then he looked up at the line of faces at the ship's rail. They were faces as ravaged as the ship itself: maniac faces. Mr. Soutar, a length of iron pipe in his hand, was even foaming at the mouth: a fleck blew from his lips and slanted into the sea, where it floated. Dick felt the rage of his companions fill him; he too was trembling with rage. All these men, to board *their* ship!

In Hazard

". . . Stay where you are," Captain Abraham said quietly to his men, and climbed the ladder alone.

He passed through the silent guard: who took no notice of him, their eyes never leaving for a moment the boat below; only Mr. Buxton followed him, and he climbed to the lower bridge.

There the two Captains met: and shook hands.

"I congratulate you, Captain," said the stranger.

"Thank you," said Edwardes. "Come into my cabin."

So the three of them entered the captain's cabin. Captain Edwardes produced a bottle of gin from a cupboard, doing the honours as host. Each took a ceremonial sip.

After that, they talked business: signed Lloyd's contract. The destination was to be Belize, in British Honduras.

Captain Edwardes now looked sane enough: so Abraham ventured to ask him: "Why won't you allow my men on board?"

Edwardes turned red as a colonel, his neck swelling over his collar.

"I allow no man on board without my permission."

"Why?" said Abraham bluntly: "Have you got an infectious disease on board?"

"If I refuse permission, no man on earth has a right to ask my reason!" cried Edwardes, thumping the table.

"Well, I'm in charge of salvaging this vessel, and I insist on having my men!"

"Your men can work for you on your own ship, they won't work on mine!" said Captain Edwardes.

Abraham rose to his feet: "Then I shall tear up this contract," he said.

"You can tear up your own copy if you like," said Edwardes: "but I don't tear up my copy, and you have signed it."

Captain Abraham was bewildered: simply did not know what to do. After all, *he* was responsible that the towing line was properly fixed. His own men were experts at the job, it was their business. These lunatic scarecrows! How could he rely on them to do it? And besides, his human heart told him that what these men needed was rest, not more work.

"Captain Edwardes," he said: "do you imagine that if I use my own men it's going to affect the salvage claim?"

A flicker of Edwardes's eyes betrayed that one nail at least was hit on the head. But he answered in a strangled voice:

"I'll have you know, Captain, that anything needful on this ship my own men can do. We don't need any help from strangers to work our own ship, *thank you*—what do you think my men are? Passengers?"

This was no ordinary situation, to be dealt with by cold logic. Such high-pitched emotion could only be answered in the same key. Captain Abraham rose from his seat, moved into the centre of the cabin, and there fell on both his knees. He lifted his right hand above his head, fixed his worldly, hatchet-face in as other-worldly an expression as he could manage:

"Captain!" he said, "I swear by Almighty God, that if I have my own men on board to fix the tow it shall not affect the salvage question not by one jot nor one tittle! Nor it don't derogate any from your crew! I swear by Almighty God that it's just the usual procedure!"

"Very well," said Captain Edwardes, a tear in his eye: "Mr. Buxton, let them come up."

It is an uncommon sight nowadays, that: to see one captain, in his uniform, kneeling in another captain's cabin.

III

They took the "Archimedes's" towing wire, and passing the eye over one of her bits made a great loop, bringing the wire back to the same bit and securing it. Then they carried it across the deck, and made a similar bridle on the other bow. With an enormous iron shackle they fastened a heavy manila cable into these two loops jointly: and towing began. What steam the "Archimedes" still possessed was turned on to her steering gear. For it makes a big difference if the vessel being towed can steer. Otherwise she will sheer about: and it is that, often as not, which snaps the tow-line, or even turns the tow right over.

The men from the "Patricia" treated the "Archimedes's" men with courtesy and respect. Partly this was a natural feeling—honouring men who have achieved something stupendous, and to have lived through these five days was itself stupendous. Partly it was like the oriental's respect for the madman. They had not forgotten their welcome— those scowling faces, those menacing clubs. You had to mind your eye with these chaps— Yes, sir!

Captain Abraham, guessing that catering on the "Archimedes" might present difficulties, had the supper for his sixteen men cooked on his own ship, and sent across. When it arrived, the "Archimedes's" men never thought for a moment it was not meant for them: they gathered round and wolfed it in two shakes. The "Patricia's" took it very well— raised no protest as they saw their supper going. God, how those men ate! They must be short of food.

So then Captain Abraham enquired, and Captain Edwardes admitted it: yes, they were a bit short of food, and drink. Captain Abraham, secretly ashamed that he had not enquired before, sent across a small supply of provisions and water to the "Archimedes." But he could not send over much, or he would have run short himself.

In Hazard

It was in the late afternoon, not long before sunset, that Dick descried an island, almost right ahead. It was Swan Island: one of a lonely little pair a hundred miles from the nearest other land. Edwardes was heartily glad the storm had dropped him when it did, had not driven him on that island. For no tidal wave in the world could have lifted them over the sixty-foot line of cliffs that for half a mile fringe the eastern side.

Ordinarily, these cliffs are crowned with trees—for it is a guano island, plaguy fertile. But as they drew near, Captain Edwardes noticed the trees were gone. The brow of the cliff was bald as a roughly plucked chicken, and showing the same occasional broken stumps.

Captain Edwardes scanned it with his binoculars.

"Seem to have caught it a bit on land, too," he said to Captain Abraham.

"I'll say they have!" said Captain Abraham. "We're darned lucky to be at sea. The hurricane hit Cuba last night—just the western end. Do you know Santa Lucia?—No, I guess you wouldn't: it's a little coasting port in the Canal di Guaniguanicos. Only small craft ever put in there: one of the old buccaneering hide-outs, I've been told. I had a radio this morning. A tidal wave hit the town, and drowned two thousand people. That's about all there was living there, I should reckon. Washed it right out."

(That same tidal wave which, by lifting them over the reefs had saved their lives!)

"And we haven't lost a man!" said Captain Edwardes: "Captain, the Lord our God is very merciful!"

Captain Abraham cleared his throat in an embarrassed way.

By the time they passed the islands, at their slow pace, it was dark—too dark to see how the guano station on the western island had fared. But there were no lights to be seen.

IV

The officers ate their share of the supper in the saloon, as usual: but all somehow crowded round two tables, since the third was smashed. Deck and engine-room mixed at last.

Dick could not get the memory of that Chinaman he had arrested out of his head: so that he ventured to ask the Captain:

"That Chinaman, Sir, you ordered under arrest: what is going to be done with him?"

"He'll be sent back to Hongkong. Then I expect he'll be extradited to Canton, by the Chinese authorities."

"And then, Sir?"

Captain Edwardes pulled an imaginary trigger in the air.

"Good God alive!" Dick dropped his fork, suddenly unable to eat.

In Hazard

Captain Edwardes sighed.

"I don't like it either," he said: "but we have our duty to do. And I don't think you need waste any pity on him. He's a bandit—that means he has probably murdered and tortured countless innocent people."

Dick sat silent, all the missionary stories of Chinese tortures that he had ever read rising in his mind. Could this decent-looking fireman have really done them? Toasted babies? Cut off old men's eyelids, and buried them up to the neck in sand? And that one with the ants (he could not remember quite how it is done)?

Perhaps he had. You can't tell by an oriental's face whether he is wicked or not—not like an Englishman.

But he was so light—he couldn't weigh more than seven stone.

"Dinna alloo your min' tae dwell on it, Mr. Watchett," Mr. MacDonald broke in. "Shootin' is naught tae a Chinaman. They dinna min' daith, whit way a whit' mon min's it. It's a scienteefic fack that a Chinaman has fewer nairves in his body than whit we ha'e; they canna feel pain. Nearer beasts than men, they are!"

MacDonald rose, and went out onto the deck, walking aft to the shattered poop.

The pumping of the after hold had raised her stern a little, but on the lower side the sea still seemed very close. Leaning on a bit of rail, Mr. MacDonald gazed at the sea. The sky was thick with a multitude of stars, of all ranges of brilliance. The water broke in phosphorescence, their faint streaming replica. Aft, a white light at last winked out on the island astern of them.

The luminous water flowed by like a river.

How he hated the water! Hated it as if it had been another man. But now he was saved from it: it would not drown him this time. Thereupon Mr. MacDonald made a vow to himself, that it should not get another chance. He would retire. True, he had meant to wait another year or two. But these days had aged him more than a year or two. And he had a bit of money laid by, in the bank: enough to live on. True, the bairns had not finished their schooling. Well, if Jean wanted to go to High-school she must work for scholarships, the same as he had. He had earned a rest.

He turned his back on the hated sea: climbed onto the rail and sat there, like a boy. He began to think of the paradise-life he would lead, when he had retired from the sea. Some trim-clipt bushes, with a neatly swept path between. There in Gloucestershire? True, it was far from the sea. But mebbe he would go back near his old home, in Dumbartonshire.

Now that he had firmly resolved to leave the sea, that little hard, feverish knot in his mind, whose continual spinning had kept him for five days and nights from even a wink of sleep, seemed to dissolve. There was a pool of sleep in his mind, in which it melted fast. Suddenly—with no warning at all—deep sleep overcame him: and he fell off the rail backwards into the sea.

The shock of the water, of course, woke him, and he swam for quite a time.

Chapter XIV

Dick's mind was rather deeply affected by the arrest of Ao Ling: and neither the Captain nor Mr. MacDonald had really relieved him. Like most white young men, he had not really looked on the Chinese as human until he had touched one. In consequence, the shock of that touch had been much greater than it would have been in the case of another white man. If he had been grappling with a white man, he would have known what to expect, in the way of feel: whereas the feel of Ao Ling took him quite by surprise.

Moreover, Ao Ling was the first man he had ever knocked out: he was not prepared for what a satisfying pleasure that can be.

But it is the curious mood that succeeded this satisfactory instant which puzzles me. Why should he have found the feel of Ao Ling, as he carried him to the hospital, so curiously reminiscent of the feel of Sukie, as he carried her to the sofa?

In Hazard

Was it just because they were much the same weight, and both had smooth skins?

Whatever the reason, he could not get the man's fate out of his mind, he kept going over it, again and again: was inordinately concerned about it. It fell to his lot to accompany the Captain and the doctor on their inspection, the next morning. His heart beat rather wildly, at the thought of seeing Ao Ling face to face. What would a man who is going to be executed look like? Surely he would not look like other men: certain death must surely set its seal beforehand on a face. And what would Ao Ling feel, when he saw the man who had seized him? Who had set his wheels, as it were, on the track that ran straight down to death?

Ao Ling was sitting on the bed, when they came in: his elbows on his knees, his manacled hands supporting his chin. His straight black hair stood forward from his forehead. Only the flat nose, the habitually parted lips, really showed. But he looked up: saw Dick's curiously inquisitive gaze fastened on him. He had in fact no memory at all of whose sudden blow had felled him. He stared back, in surprise.

Dick stared as if his eyes were gimlets. But he could make nothing of the Chinaman's expression. Stare, stare.—But how could those two young men see beyond each other's eyes? They were both the same age; and in some ways, very similar.

210

But their upbringings had been very different.

Now their prospects for the future, it seemed, were rather different also.

II

Later in the morning, as Dick was trying to get some order among the possessions in his room, he was seized with a complete change of mood: a feeling of dramatic pride, like what he felt when he was oiling in the forward latrine. It is not every young man who has overcome a notorious Chinese bandit with his bare hands—knocked him out, handcuffed him, and carried him bodily to prison. For that, after all, is what he had done, when you put it into plain words without any trimmings (so why add the trimmings?).

It was a pity, in a way, that he had no souvenir of it. The Colonel has a tiger-skin on the hall floor: you trip over the thing, and he launches easily into the story of how he shot it. It is a pity that when you arrest a murderer there are no horns or anything you can keep, to get the story started (I am sure it would stimulate our police in making arrests if they knew that the judge, when it was all over, would send them, suitably mounted, the "mask").

And yet it was curious, if Ao Ling really was a bandit and a murderer, that his face did not look more fiendish. Of course, villains can cover their wickedness with a look of the utmost benevolence:

211

but not, surely, for ever. At the moment of arrest
—that, according to Dick's reading-matter, was
when the innocent look should have dropped, a
look of baffled and fiendish cruelty should have
contorted the man's features. But instead of that
Dick could not, for the life of him, remember any
other look than one of silly surprise.

Dick sought out Dr. Frangcon, and questioned
him. Was Ao Ling really a bandit? The doctor
knew Chinamen better than anyone else on board.

Dr. Frangcon listened seriously and rather
sadly.

"How can I tell?" he said. "Also, it is not my
job—and it is not your job. He certainly came on
board with false papers. That alone makes it our
duty to arrest him and hand him over to the police.
What else he has done is their business, not ours."

That sounded logical. But an illogical voice in
Dick insisted on urging still, that if you give over
a man to be shot dead you have at least a measure
of responsibility in the matter.

He found himself suddenly remembering the
little girl laid out flat on the trolley.

III

Captain Abraham left his own vessel in charge of
his Chief Officer: as long as any of his sixteen
men remained on board the "Archimedes," he intended to stay there with them. He could trust
them, up to a point: they had behaved with great

patience up to now. But it would not take more
than a spark, he knew, to start a fight. And when
men in the condition of the "Archimedes's" men
fight, they fight to kill and without thought of
fair play.

Captain Abraham observed the condition of the
"Archimedes's" men very carefully: it was part of
his job, and he would probably be expected to
furnish, in the strictest confidence, a report on
them. Captain Edwardes, he thought, did not seem
very greatly affected, now the incident of the board-
ing-party was over. He seemed worried, increas-
ingly worried: not like a man bowled over by
anything past, but rather like a man with an
anxious ordeal ahead of him. Captain Abraham
guessed easily what that was. The Enquiry which
would presently take place into his every minutest
action and motive throughout the whole storm was
not a thing which any master would look forward
to. Captain Abraham had been a witness at many
such Enquiries. He knew what a tendency there is
for the experts, with all the facts before them, with
wisdom after the event, to declare unjustly but in
all honesty that a man has acted wrongly. Nothing
is harder than to bear in mind, when conducting
such an Enquiry, only the knowledge that was
available to the Master at each time his decisions
had to be made: to rule out completely from the
reckoning indications which came to light even, it
may be, only a few minutes later.

In Hazard

That Captain Edwardes was fortunate in his officers, and especially in Mr. Buxton and Mr. Rabb, Abraham also decided. They were a sound pair, those two: unemotional and efficient. Men on whom you could well rely. Of the two, it was Rabb who showed least signs of wear and tear. And yet there was something very odd about him. He carried out all his duties with meticulous efficiency; but he seemed to avoid his fellow-officers: he seemed to have a grievance against them. Captain Abraham wondered what it was.

When they all gathered in the saloon for lunch, Captain Abraham continued his observation: but you would not have guessed it by his manner. He was telling stories. And not stories of storms at sea, either.

Mr. MacDonald's chair of course was empty. But only the two captains and the doctor and Mr. Soutar knew that he was missing. They gave it out that he had had a breakdown, and had been transferred to the "Patricia." For it never entered their heads that he had fallen overboard: they thought he had jumped. And once jumping begins it is likely to go on. Best keep it quiet for the present.

Captain Abraham's stories merged from one into another: but nobody listened much.

Things were nearly back to normal, now. Already the carpenters had replaced the missing table, and Deck and Engine-room were sorted out again. The Chief Steward presided in his pantry;

and two yellow waiters, in clean jackets, ceremoni-
ously served the dishes.

A ships's saloon is never a very talkative place,
but this one was more silent than usual: that is
probably the only difference you would have noticed: and Captain Abraham's stories went on
and on.

Presently he ran out of stories, with no-one to
cap them: so for want of anything better to say he
began to describe Belize (none of them had ever
seen the place, not even Edwardes).

"Ha'n't you put in there before, Captain? No?
Well, it's not a bad berth, in the dry season. It's no
Shanghai, mind you: it's a quiet little place. But
it's a purty sight, as you come into harbour—that
is, if you like old-fashioned places, same as me:
peepin' out of the palms and oleanders, with the
mountains dim and hazy in the distance, and the
sea dotted with little cays and islands like . . .
like . . ."

His voice tailed away: he could not think what
they were like, except cays and islands: and
nobody seemed to care.

—That was an idea, Dick thought: suppose he
was to let the Chinaman loose, when they reached
Belize? The man would not have a very good
chance, perhaps; but he *might* get away. At the
least he would have a run for his money. At the
thought of stealing to the cell quietly in the night,
and letting the man go, a feeling of pleasurable

215

warmth suffused Dick's body: the thought of Ao Ling's unspoken gratitude. Of meeting him, perhaps years later, in some desperate fracas in Central China, when all seemed lost: of Ao Ling recognising him, and saving his life in turn (for a Chinaman never forgets).

"It's a swampy sort of ground," Captain Abraham went on inexorably: "most of the houses stand on mahogany pillars. They're all wood of course, I mean the houses, you know; with jalousies: they stand up on short mahogany masts. Time was, when the mahogany trade was flourishing, it was a rich little port—for mahogany's what they chiefly produce there. Niggers cut it, up in the forests, where no white man can live, and float it down the river in rafts. But I hear tell now mahogany's gone out of fashion, or something. The trade isn't a tenth of what it was. Terrible poverty. It's the niggers themselves comes floating down the river now, more than the timber. That's a funny thing! Some bright young spark over in Europe says, 'No more heavy old mahogany for me,' meaning no harm: but what's the result? Sure as houses, presently down the river they come, those niggers, floating dead!

"Now, I *like* a nice bit of mahogany, myself, to eat my dinner off."

Dick imagined the Chinaman slipping away quietly in the night; and then next day the hue and cry. Emaciated negroes with their tom-toms, hunting him for the blood-money. The Chinaman splashing desperately through swamps: lashed at by snakes: tripped by creepers: plunging ever deeper into the jungle: and all the time the police inexorably closing in . . . it was just as enthralling a picture as the other one.

"—Belize is the capital, you know. Got a hospital there. And a gaol and barracks on the north side, across the river from Government House."

Suddenly one of the engineers pushed back his chair, and dropped his dark head in his hands.

"She's sinking! I know she's sinking!" he cried out in a loud voice.

There was a frightful hush, broken only by his sobs. Then Soutar and the Third took him, one by each arm, and led him away, with Dr. Frangcon following.

"—The only brick buildings on the *South* Bank, so far as I am aware," Captain Abraham went on in a slightly louder voice, "are St. John's Church, and the Wesley Chapel. There're a number of them on the North Bank, of course."

But then his eye caught the apprentices' table, and again he faltered and stopped. All three apprentices were silently crying—the tears pouring down their faces. Not one of them seemed to notice he was doing it himself, for each kept pointing at the other two—asking people to look at *their* condition, and do something for *them*. Each one seemed to think he was all right himself.

When Mr. Buxton saw this, he suddenly burst into tears too.

Just then Dr. Frangcon came back, and dosed everyone with bromide—well or ill. Everyone in the room.

But what had riveted Captain Abraham's attention had not been the tears of Bennett, or Phillips: it was the third boy. For he was wearing Captain Abraham's own gold watch.

Captain Abraham clapped his hand to his waistcoat pocket. He had never, till that moment, noticed it was gone.

IV

Night fell: and those who were not on watch retired, with a second dose of bromide, to their bunks.

Captain Edwardes undressed fully for the first time, and got into pyjamas: lit a pipe and rolled into his bunk. The ship was still listed, of course: lucky the lower side of the bed was against the wall, or he could never have stayed in it.

As Captain Abraham had guessed, he was mortally worried about the future. But in a way, it was not so much himself he was worried about as the Owners. He did hope they would not make fools of themselves. A very good feeling had been built up, these last twenty years, between the Office and the Fleet: he hoped they would not jeopardise that. If the Enquiry found, on good and sufficient grounds, that he had been deficient in seamanship —well, let them sack him. But let them do it quickly: the other officers would respect that. On the other hand, if the Enquiry found that he was not seriously at fault, let them say so, and re-instate him at once. No shilly-shallying. No setting him to coasting for six months, on the pretence that it was for the good of his health, while they made up their minds. Better sack him unjustly than that.

Captain Edwardes knew very well the sort of verdict that an excess of justice might lead them into. They might fine him for running his ship into danger, and give him a gold watch for getting her out again. Well, perhaps that *was* what he deserved. But it would not look well—not to the rest of the Fleet: not to the World.

A presentation gold watch. He could imagine the scene. He would have to make a speech. Captain Edwardes's Welsh blood tingled with pleasure at the thought of making a speech, before all those big-wigs. But at the moment he could only think of one thing to say:

"Gentlemen," he imagined himself saying, as he held up the trophy: "My Lord Mayor and Gentlemen! This watch will be to me a perpetual memento of the wrath of Heaven."

Through the door of his state-room, he heard the sound of a stealthy movement in the cabin beyond. Someone was in there who had no business to be! Edwardes lay still and quiet, listening with all his ears.

There was a rustling of papers: then a glass fell to the floor. He drew up his muscles, ready to spring out of bed suddenly. There was a soft *plop* onto the floor—and Thomas poked his inquisitive little snout in through the door, asking if he might come in. He looked no thinner than usual but ruffled; his coat staring, as if he really did want someone to care for him.

Captain Edwardes reached out an arm, and took the little creature up into his bed, and fondled him.

Rabb. That was a ticklish business. If he told the whole truth in his report, it was the street for Rabb. The man was an efficient and popular officer; a clean-living man. He had broken down in the storm, that was true. But that was bad luck. A man has no right to have to face such a storm as that. He might have gone through his whole career without ever a fault, if he had not been so unlucky as to have to face that storm. The odds were heavily against his ever having, in his career, to face such a storm again. Perhaps, too, if he had been in his own ship, with his own prescribed duty to do, just that slight enhancement of his responsibility might have held him together.

An efficient officer: broken through one piece of bad luck.

Tuesday

Captain Edwardes toyed with the idea of saying nothing whatever about Rabb, in his report . . . but in his heart of hearts he knew he could not do it.

Soutar, now Acting-Chief, turned in also for a long night: for in his new capacity he was excused watch-keeping. And there was little enough in the engine-room to do. Already most of the mess was cleared up. There was no very real damage done down there—lucky, really, the engines had been stopped before anything had smashed.

Soutar turned off the light, and went to sleep. But he did not sleep for long. He heard someone calling him: and then saw Mr. MacDonald's eyes glaring into his.

"In the Next Worrld Man casts Reason, Mr. Soutar, as I tau'd ye!" he said. That must be true: for his face was wholly and voluntarily mad: and in place of his grey moustache he wore the long black moustachios of the traditional mandarin.

Soutar gave a strangled shout: sat up, and turned on the light. MacDonald was gone: but Soutar felt no inclination to sleep again. He sat up, and began to read a book. It was by Ethel M. Dell.

Mr. Rabb, before turning in, took a manicure set, and with the little clippers began to pare the cuticle round his nails. He could never cut the nails themselves, because they were always too close bitten. But he was in the habit of paring the cuticle, and polishing the backs of the nails themselves with a little pad. A gentleman is known by his hands.

His mind was quite made up. Captain and Mate had conspired against him. Ever since he had disapproved of their dancing, at Norfolk, he had known by small indications that they meant to do him down. The Wicked are like that: they will never face a Christian openly, they do him down behind his back.

This was their chance. Because, in that awful storm he had used a little discretion, had refused to walk into the traps they had laid to kill him, they would send in a report on him that would get him sacked. Actually they had been just as frightened as he was: for instance, hadn't he seen Captain Edwardes himself in a panic in the wheelhouse, when he thought the Bridge was going? But if he reported that, on his bare word who would believe him?

The orders David gave Bathsheba's husband were nothing to the orders they had kept on giving him! If he had obeyed one of these orders he would have been a dead man—which was what they wanted, of course. Well, instead he was a live one. But they had him, just the same.

He might write to the Chairman and explain

the plot, perhaps: but it was hardly likely his word would count for much against both of theirs.

Well, he was not going to give them the chance. At Belize he would leave the ship. But he would not join the "Descartes." They couldn't touch him then! And he would not be long out of a job. There were companies who would jump at the chance of securing a man who had served in the famous Sage Line.

Dick Watchett also could not sleep. His face felt hot, and his brain lively. He was thinking over the scene at lunch that day. That engineer had broken down. The boys had broken down. He had even seen Mr. Buxton crying! Mr. Buxton! While he himself had felt not the slightest inclination to break down. He was stronger than them.

This surprised him: but it gave him immense confidence for the future. He had gone into the storm a boy: he was now a man. A sailor, a hard case. He had faced, for the first time in his life, the prolonged danger of death: and it had not broken him, he had got used to it. Frankly, he did not care now *what* further dangers he faced.

As for that Chinaman, how odd that he had been so concerned about him! Let him die. There are plenty of Chinamen in the world: one less makes no odds. Yes, it was better that he should die: it rounded the story off more satisfactorily. On the other hand, if he helped him escape at Belize, helped him slip through the Captain's fingers— well, there was something of a thrill in that . . .

Dick imagined himself meeting Sukie: what she would think of him now. *He* would not tell her his adventures, of course: someone else would have already done that. Probably it would be in the papers, and she would devour every paragraph, and then some shipmate would meet her and tell her about the Chinese bandit: how Dick had downed him with his bare hands, and how presently the man had been executed for his awful crimes . . . or, some shipmate would tell her about the young Chinaman, how Dick had arrested him at the Captain's orders, and then, knowing him innocent, had dared everything to help him escape . . . well, it was hard yet to make up his mind which.

But all the time, as he imagined Sukie—a chastened, adoring Sukie—fawning round his heroic person, there was something in his mind growing more insistent, like a trickle of cold water down the neck. Suddenly it burst out into the light of discovery: all this was very little use to him, because he was no longer in love with Sukie at all! After all, she was only a High-school kid—and he was a grown man. A skinny little bit at that, with no more brains in her head than a pigeon! What use was her homage to him?

And so the man, Dick Watchett, the hard case, turned over placidly to go to sleep: yet conscious all the while that something had left him which he regretted.

But it has to be like that. A man cannot stretch the gamut of his emotions, he can only shift it. If you reach out at one end, to cover the emotion of danger of death, till you can cope with that comfortably, you can't expect to keep a delicate sensitiveness the other end too. Just like there are baritones, tenors, trebles: but no one can sing the whole length of the piano. It was as if Dick's voice had broken now. He had some fine new manly notes. But the old top-notes were gone.

Not, perhaps, for good: the shift had been artificial. In time, security might restore him to his natural range. And time, too, might blunt the edge of his re-awakened belief in God: the edge of which was at present uncomfortably sharp. But I will say no more of Dick Watchett: perhaps I have already said too much, about one who after all was a very normal young man.

V

Only one man on the whole ship was at this time already sound asleep: and that was Ao Ling. There was no light in his prison, so he fell asleep soon after sunset: and lay there, on his side, on the hospital cot, his handcuffed hands between his knees.

He was surprised to find a Fukienese girl on the cot beside him. He raised himself on one elbow, to embrace her: but the fine hair on her face and hands warned him that she was but a fox in human shape.

Moreover, he saw to his horror that she was in labour: the pains came on her at that moment. Deeply embarrassed, he would have left the cot; but he found that he could not rise. So he rolled over, turned his face away from her.

Then a voice said "Look!"

The room was filled with a red light, and a peculiar smell: and a ball of white flesh was rolling on the floor like a wheel. Ao Ling leant over the side of the cot (for the fox-girl had now vanished) with his knife in his hand; and as it passed he slashed it open. A small manikin emerged, surrounded in a halo of red light. It was Captain Edwardes, in a pair of silk Chinese trousers, from which flashed dazzling rays of gold light. He strutted up and down, growing bigger all the time.

In the deep silence something was singing: and Ao Ling turned his head just in time to see a black-bearded porpoise, dangling on a fishing-line, singing like mad. Then the line tautened, whizzing it up into the sky.

Ao Ling looked up, and saw above him an immense figure riding on a black unicorn: a figure with a green face and fluffy crimson hair, and a cyclops-eye from which flashed a pure white beam. He held in his hand a fishing-rod: and on the line the father-porpoise still dangled, still singing.

Round them the sea roared and heaved: but out of it rose a single tree. Its leaves were of white jade. Its trunk was about as thick round as a man could clasp; and up the middle ran a transparent tube of pale yellow. The foliage was dense, and tinkled when a leaf fell. But now it was lightning-riven: and caught in the cleft was a blue-faced bat-winged duke, hollering in agony with his enormous monkey-mouth and hammering incessantly on the drums which were hung about him.

Captain Edwardes by now had grown a beard like the porpoise's. But he drew a dart from his belt and flung it at the figure on the unicorn. It snatched the yelling demon from the tree, and yelling also vanished in the clouds.

A great mouth rose out of the water, as wide and as deep as a well, against which the waves could be heard splashing. Captain Edwardes drew another dart from his waist and flung it at the mouth: and with a blasty breath that drove the ship sideways through the water it too vanished.

But the sea, where was the sea? No longer any water, only the seething of innumerable dragons. How welcome they were! Each had a fifth foot growing from his navel, and no black beards under their long snouts. They flailed with their shaggy legs and lashed their hairy tails.

Then one dragon, in a fine armour of golden-glowing scales, flung itself onto the ship, and crawled up the sloping deck. As it moved the deck was depressed with its weight, like a tent-roof when a cat walks upon it. Its forehead projected over its blazing eyes: its ears were small and thick: its tongue was long, and its teeth were sharp.

But Captain Edwardes drew from his trousers thousands of balls of fire, which flew from his hands and struck it, so that it lay cowering down. Then the Captain straddled over it, cruelly tearing off its scales one by one, so that it cried in agony, shrinking all the time smaller and smaller, and at last weeping with the hopeless, shuddering sobs of a despairing child.

The voice was his own infantile voice, weeping to him out of the far years of the past.

VI

They were in the open sea, now, heading for the Gulf of Honduras; more than a hundred miles from any land. Ahead lay the small black silhouette of the "Patricia," her smoke seen only as a black blank in the myriad of stars, three vertical lights at her mast-head. Between, the tow-rope dipped occasionally in the water; then lifted, dripping trickling phosphorescent drops along its whole length.

Next came the jagged bows of the "Archimedes," still tip-tilted over to one side. Right up in the peak the look-out stood, occasionally shifting his position from side to side. Presently he came aft a little, and rang six bells: the only bells ever tolled over the grave of Mr. Ramsay Mac-Donald, once a chief engineer.

FINIS

Library of Congress Cataloguing in Publication Data

Hughes, Richard Arthur Warren, 1900-1976.
In hazard.
Reprint. Originally published: New York: Time, 1966.
I. Title.
PR6015.U3515 1982   823'.912   82-3286 AACR2
ISBN 0-8094-3729-5 (deluxe)
ISBN 0-8094-3730-9 (pbk.)